JOB FOR TEENS

by

Marc Bastawrous

ST SHENOUDA'S PRESS
SYDNEY, AUSTRALIA
2019

Job for Teens

ST SHENOUDA PRESS
8419 Putty Rd,
Putty, NSW, 2330

www.stshenoudapress.com

ISBN 13: 978-0-6482814-6-7

About the Author:

Marc Bastwarous is currently studying medicine at Bond university. He attends St Mark's Coptic Orthodox Church, Sydney where he is heavily involved in youth ministry and sunday school. He is a regular blogger on the Upper Room media app. He writes about many topics relating to the Orthodox faith.

Typesetting: Anthony Bebawi

Cover Design:
Mariana Hanna
In and Out Creation Pty Ltd
inandoutcreations.com.au

Text Layout:
Hani Ghaly,
Begoury Graphics
begourygraphics@gmail.com

CONTENTS

INTRODUCTION

Before beginning this book, let's make one thing very clear: The book of Job has the potential to be extremely boring. It is repetitive in its theme and it can sometimes feel as though it is just one endless, frustrating argument between 4 old men. In fact, I was once asked by a friend to join them in reading a passage from the bible each night. Let's call this friend 'Joey'. Joey wanted to start sharing one verse from each chapter of the bible we would read together at night so that we could encourage each other to be more consistent with our bible reading. And so, we did that. We worked our way through all 14 letters of St Paul, a couple of the gospels, even some of the Old Testament classics like Esther and Jonah. All in all, it was over a year that we continued to motivate each other to read. Then we thought it would be nice to start the book of Job. It was during this book that our relationship ended. I haven't received a bible verse from Joey since. The book became too much for us to handle, we both got bored.

However, since studying this book, I've found it to be riddled with treasures. The book of Job answers so many of life's unanswered questions. 'Why does evil exist? Why does a good God allow suffering? How should I respond to tribulations?' It is poetic and powerful in equal measure and I pray that its beauty can be even somewhat translated through this book.

7

CONTEXT

The book of Job is regarded as one of the
wisdom books found in the Old Testament, fit
for all times and all people. It speaks of the
sufferings of a blessed man by the name of
Job who has to deal with many tribulations
as well as the accusations of his friends. In
all this, Job maintains his love for God even
though he loses patience with his sufferings
and challenges the command of God towards
the end of the book. It can be a very confusing
book due to the many different characters
and the excessive dialogue but the message is
still made very clear and the book is very easily
relatable to as a result. In these final chapters
the Lord, who had been silent throughout
the trials of Job previously, speaks up and
questions Job regarding the secrets of the
universe to which Job has no response.
God, in the midst of Job's anguish, revealed
Himself to him to show that He is the one in
charge and Job, being the weak human that
he is, will not understand why God is dealing
with him in this way. In this manner, Job is a
character that we can very easily relate to as
we learn how to deal with pain and misery in
the world while we continue in our spiritual
struggle and trying to keep faith in God. At
times when it feels like we've hit rock bottom
it may be hard to see God working in our lives
but as we learn through the life of Job, it's the
times that are darkest when God chooses to
reveal His light.

> **What the Fathers Say**
>
> This is what
> we learn from
> Job's case. God
> puts those who
> can endure
> temptations
> even to death,
> as a role model
> before
> the weak
>
> – St. Basil
> the Great

PURPOSE & THEME

> **What the Fathers Say**
>
> *Grief is intentionally given to us; to cure us of sin.*
>
> *– St. John Chrysostom*

Whilst it may not be clear throughout the book, there are several indications regarding the purpose behind the writing of this book. It is a common misconception that sufferings come as God's punishment for your individual sins, as the friends of Job try to tell him, and so this book aims to reveal that God's rule over humanity cannot be assumed by a simple formula understood by the tiny human mind. Sin does not always lead to bad consequences and in the same way, righteousness does not always produce a positive outcome, which is the major teaching found in this book. God is an unlimited being, so for us to try and understand Him and His plans with our limited minds is a fault in itself. So, just as Job comes to learn at the end of this book, we must leave things in the hands of God trusting that no matter the path we may take, it is for our own good. The book presents to us Job, as a living example, of someone who had a lot of love for God and who trusted in His care.

The themes that are touched upon in this book match with its purpose and message that it attempts to express; that the infinite wisdom of the Lord cannot be understood by the human mind. Daily we are confronted with situations that are similar to that of Job's, although most likely not to that difficulty. However, it is worthwhile and helpful to read this book and be made known to the wisdom of God as we learn to grant Him control over our lives, in all circumstances. No doubt all our lives will be shaped in their own unique way, our reaction to different situations will depend though on whom we choose to place our trust in. Will we choose to trust in our own wisdom, the wisdom of others or the wisdom of God? We must learn from the story of Job to trust in the unlimited and infinite knowledge of God so that we can say with Saint Augustine, "I do not know what the future holds, but it is enough my beloved Lord, to know You are near defending me."

AUTHORSHIP & CONTEXT

The author of the book of Job has often been disputed amongst scholars and other interpreters of the Bible. The story is set outside of Israel, in the land of Edom, so the historical accounts found in the Old Testament cannot be used to determine an exact time period in which it was written, making it more difficult to figure out the author. However, some interpreters suggest that the use of old Jewish names of "Eloah" and "Shaddai" from the book seem to fit best in the age of Abraham, Isaac and Jacob meaning it was written during their time. Other scholars believe the book was written by Moses, who used it to comfort his people in slavery by teaching them, through this story, that the Lord will eventually rescue them from their sufferings as He did with Job. The most likely author however is Job himself, as very personal thoughts and very accurate dialogue and timing is written throughout the whole book so it seems more likely that it

> **What the Fathers Say**
>
> We know from several sources that nothing would ever happen without the will of God. He, who believes that God is the Reason, the Wisdom, the perfect Goodness, and the Truth; And that He would never allow for anything bad to happen to us; would realize that there would be no factor of chance nor chaos in God's ordinances... They would be always convenient for us. We should know that all things happen for the best
>
> – St. Gregory of Nyssa

would have been Job, who went through this tribulation, to have written the book.

What the Fathers Say

> Through all those temptations, Satan did not get any benefit; whereas 'Job' alone got all the benefit, because he endured with perseverance
>
> — Fr Theodore

STRUCTURE

The book of Job is not merely an Old Testament tale, but it is also one of the greatest pieces of literature in all of history. The writer has purposely designed the book in a poetic way, where the conflict is shown at the beginning and, after a long development of thoughts and entertaining discussions, is resolved at the end. The author does this whilst masterfully shifting away from the story in chapter 28 to deliver a poem in honor of wisdom; specifically, the wisdom of God.

The narrator begins the book by emphasizing the righteousness of Job on more than one occasion in chapter 1 and describes him to be a wealthy and prosperous man. The enemy, the devil, then challenges God, who believes in the righteousness of Job, to test the sincerity of his commitment to God by asking to bring disaster to him and his household. The Lord grants the enemy his request at which point he begins to inflict havoc on his life in all aspects.

The poetic portion of this book begins with the lamentations of Job in the two chapters following his demise, before a drawn-out saga of speeches and arguments begins amongst Job and his friends between chapters 4 and 27, where his friends try to advise Job on how he should resolve his miserable condition with the Lord. It is during this part of the story where we see Job's resilience and pride being tested as he tries to maintain his innocence and integrity before his friends.

So as to not lose sight of the main theme of the book, the author interrupts and writes a beautiful piece of poetry in chapter 28 that highlights the fear of God as being the foundation of wisdom. This allows us, the readers, to refocus our attention on the major theme of the book in the middle of the arguing between Job and his friends.

Job continues to plead his case, before a young man by the name of Elihu interferes and offers his opinion to provide insight from the perspective of a youth. Again, his words are met with no reward before God breaks His silence in the final chapters of the book and teaches Job that, whilst he may be innocent, he does not understand the ways of the Lord and how He deals with His beloved children.

The epilogue, the final chapter 42, speaks of the retribution of Job and his return to righteousness as he lets go of his anger towards God before the Lord restores all that he once had and more.

The prophecies of the book of Job are read during the great Lent to prepare us for Holy week and the suffering that our Lord and Saviour Jesus Christ is to endure during this week. The Wednesday of Holy week is known as "Job's Wednesday" where the righteous Job is remembered as a representation of the Lord Jesus Christ, in his cruel sufferings as well as his final retribution. It is read specifically on the Wednesday of Holy Week as the plot against the life of Jesus started on that day signaling the beginning of His sufferings.

Job and his teachings are mentioned during the rite of Unction of the sick, to demonstrate to followers that sickness and pain are not things to be distressed over but rather an opportunity to strengthen our faith in the hands of God.

REFLECTION

Have you ever been in a situation where it felt like all hope seemed lost and God had forsaken you? Did you seek God in this time of distress? How did He respond?

CHAPTER 1

THE TRIAL BEGINS

To truly understand the book of Job, it is important to have a clear grasp on the origins of the tale. Whilst the remainder of this study on Job will only briefly explore the themes of each chapter, I thought it wise to offer a more detailed explanation of the first 3 chapters in order to appreciate the purpose that this book was written for.

Like any good book, the story of Job has a main character, the hero of the tale, otherwise known as the protagonist, and an opposing force, the antagonist. The book introduces a protagonist in Job, but not the protagonist of the book. That position will be filled later in the book by Another.

Job 1:1-3

The book of Job opens with a detailed description of all of Job's great possessions and wealth, describing him to be a very successful man in the world. His riches consisted of much land and cattle, riches in the form of money, servants to tend his home and cattle and a large family, which was considered very highly and only affordable to the wealthy in those days. However, in spite of all these great riches that he obtained on earth, the book still begins by speaking about his righteousness and fear of God saying:

"There was a man in the land of 'Uz', whose name was 'Job'; and that man was blameless and upright, and one who feared

CHAPTER 1

God and shunned evil" (Job 1: 1)

There is a clear emphasis on this righteousness on Job in the midst of all his wealth and material possessions. It is a strong reminder that God does not value us because of how wealthy we are or how successful we have become in this world, but rather He looks at our hearts and judges us based on our good works for the Kingdom of Heaven. Oftentimes we become obsessed with obtaining worldly treasures that we find ourselves neglecting the treasures that are above and inheriting the true Treasure, which is Christ and His promise of Salvation. Job here, in just the first three verses of this story, reminds us of the grace that God bestows upon those who value the heavenly kingdom above the earthly. This honour for Job did happen to come in the form of worldly gifts but only as a result of placing the laws of God higher on his pedestal. It is a valuable reminder of the words of Christ who promised, "seek first the kingdom of God and His righteousness, and all these things shall be added unto you." (Matthew 6:33).

The problem with attaching ourselves to wealth and our earthly possessions is that, we no longer have any room to attach ourselves to God. Think of it this way: it is simply not possible to hold your partners hand, if you keep your fists clenched, holding tightly onto something. In this same way, we cannot fully walk hand in hand with our Partner – Christ, until we let go of everything else.

Job 1:4-5

"Now the sons would go and feast in their houses, each on his appointed day, and would send and invite their three sisters to eat and drink with them" (Job 1: 4)

The story goes on to display a marvelous portrait of a very rich man and his children, who were not preoccupied with their wealth, as much as with gathering together with the spirit of love and unity; holding feasts in their houses, each on his appointed day, together with their three sisters; according to the words of the Psalmist: "How good and how pleasant it is, for brethren to dwell together in unity" (Psalm 133: 1). It is a form of riches we often neglect or take for granted; the wealth in fellowship. And it is interesting to note that Job played his part in the success of this fellowship by not actually attending. Some church fathers contemplate that, due to his very old age, he felt that he would be hindering the youthful nature of his children

People, Places &Things

The Land of Uz

The Land of 'Uz' is named after the son of Aram who was a direct descendant of Noah's son Shem. It is also translated the word 'oz' which means 'east,' hence suggesting that Job was "the greatest of all the people of the east."

Tearing Robes

In Jewish tradition, tearing your robe was a way of showing that you had just heard or witnessed something blasphemous. This is the same thing we see the high priest do on Good Friday during the trial of Jesus when Jesus told them that He was the "Son of God" (Mark 14:63

and interfere with their freedom by partaking in their feast. Hence, even though he may not have been present at these family feasts, he still managed to fuel the fellowship as a consequence of his wise decisions.

Job displays his love for his family in the following verse that portrays an image of him sacrificing burnt offerings on behalf of his children for fear that they may "have sinned and cursed God in their hearts," (Job 1:5). That his first priority was the salvation of his children reveals just how deeply and unconditionally he loved them. There was a saying I once heard that stated, "There is no greater love than the love that takes the name of a friend and leaves it before the throne of God in prayer." We also see here how Job did not only care for their shortcomings as far as their deeds are concerned, but even cared for their thoughts; achieving in a practical way what the Lord Christ will say in the future: "For out of the heart proceed evil thoughts... These are the things which defile a man" (Matthew 15: 19-20).

Job 1:6-12

Perhaps the greatest testament to the character of Job arrives in verse 8 of chapter 1 during a conversation between the Lord and Satan. Satan had been roaming the earth at that time seeking to cause men to stumble and fall under the power of sin when the Lord questioned him. He asked him in verse 8, "Have you considered My servant Job.

What the Fathers Say

What the The righteous in this world may not enjoy what he desires, but he may rather suffer, and be exposed to dangers; yet he eagerly waits for the coming of Christ.

– Origen

That there is none like him on the earth, a blameless and upright man, one who fears God and shuns evil?" (Job 1: 8). Can you just picture this great pride with which God spoke of His 'servant' Job? When looking to apply for a job, often you need a referee to send a letter of recommendation to enhance your chances of getting employed at that company. Now imagine your referee was God Himself, recommending you for the job you were applying for. Well, that's what happened with Job. We are all called to be servants of Christ, to fight against the enemy of God and carry our cross on our path towards salvation. God here gives Job a high commendation as His servant and speaks highly of him, stating that his righteousness and fear of God induces him to avoid evil. There are only a handful of times where God speaks this highly about anyone, others being the Centurion and John the Baptist. Thus, Job immediately joins an exclusive group of people that have received praise from the Lord and have made Him proud. How frequently do we ourselves make God proud in our day-to-day lives? More often than not we are forced to rely solely on the grace of God to protect us from the attacks of the enemy, unfit to persevere against wickedness without His defending hand.

Satan, being frustrated by his inability to break down the holiness of Job, begins to complain to God, saying that because of all the great riches and wealth that God has bestowed upon Job and due to all the protection He provides him, Job is untouchable. Satan then challenges God regarding Job saying, "But now, stretch Your hand and touch all that he has, and he will surely curse You to Your face" (Job 1: 11). What comes next is astonishing. God replies to Satan, "Behold, all that he has is in your power; only do not lay a hand on his person'. Then Satan went out from the presence of the Lord" (Job 1: 12). God removes His caring hand from Job and allows Satan full reign over his life to do as he wills because of His endless faith in His servant Job. The servant of the Lord must have full faith in the plan of God for God to have full faith in his service, as we learn from this dialogue between God and Satan. God trusted that Job would not deny Him, no matter what Satan threw in his way. He knew that this experience would only serve to strengthen the faith of Job as suffering often does in all our lives. This is similar to Peter, who was allowed to be sifted out as wheat that his faith should not fail but grow stronger (Luke 22:31-32). This same disciple Peter then went on to write in his epistle that temptations are meant to give those who manage to successfully go through them, praise, honor, and glory (1 Peter 1: 7). The devil in all his ignorance and naivety does not anticipate that when he knocks us down to our knees, we are in the perfect position to pray and plead to our Father for help. That however, is the challenge; to grow in faith through perseverance and prayer during the times of trouble. And that here is the challenge that God set for Job to accomplish.

What the Fathers Say

How could the greatness and splendor of daylight be evident, unless compared with the darkness of the night? How could some be commended for their purity; unless others are condemned for their impurity? The strong are glorified, when compared with the cowards. Sweetness is more enjoyed, after tasting what is bitter.

– Origen

Job 1:12-19

What the Fathers Say

Although he was counted as one of the richest people; But the temptation he went through proved that his only most precious possession was God.

– St. Macarius the Great

"Now there was a day when his sons and daughters were eating and drinking wine in their oldest brother's house" (Job 1: 13).

It's fascinating to see the time that Satan chose to attack Job; a time when there was complete peace, whilst his family was participating in a joyous feast. This is an interesting reminder that the devil attacks us when we least expect it, when we are so comfortable in our daily lives that even the slightest deviation from that comfort could err our faith. Immediately Job had his oxen and donkeys taken captive by raiders (1:14,15), his servants killed by the sword (1:15), his sheep and shepherds burnt and consumed by fire from heaven (1:16), his camel taken away by horsemen (1:17) and all his children killed by a great wind which caused the house they were feasting within to fall upon them (1:19). Tribulation upon tribulation came rapidly and consecutively for Job, like incessant successive waves, "Deep calls unto deep" (Psalm 42: 7), with Satan's evil plan to deny Job of any chance to think soundly; and to let him be convinced that God's wrath has dwelt upon him, and would never cease. He used the words of Job's servant, who came to inform him of all these disasters, to persuade Job that God is to blame for all the tragedies that had fell upon him all of the sudden by having him say, "The fire of God fell from heaven" (Job 1:16). Although Job had committed no major sins, and was not idle in his love and worship to God, the unwarranted fury of God would make him blaspheme Him as unjust, the plan of Satan all along. And this is something not uncommon to us. During times of severe illness, when our prayers seem to only make matters worse, we are often deluded into believing that God is not present or that He has removed His hand of protection. This causes us to think that He is unfair and leads us astray. The devil himself is not capable of creating anything only God is the Creator of things and beings. The devil only take things that already exist, mixes it with a little bit of rubbish and presents it to us in an attractive way. In this instance the sickness was the thing that was already in existence, the devil added to that the nonsense knowledge that God had forsaken the prayers of those going through the struggle and as it is always appealing for us to place blame on someone or something else during hard times, he presented God as the perfect candidate. A tactic he tried to reinforce with Job, little did he anticipate how Job would truly react.

Job 1:20-22

The response of Job to "tear his robe and shave his head" (Job 1:20) is often misunderstood as a sign of mourning, which is why when it follows that "he fell to the ground and worshipped" can at times lack sense. This was because he was in fact not in a state of mourning but rather he was retaliating 'against' the devil, not 'because' of him. Job in all his wisdom acknowledged

> ## What the Fathers Say
>
> What a sweet and brave voice! Who cannot wake up to such a voice? Who does not trust God, to walk to battle against Satan with no fear; to fight him, not with his own power, but with that of the One who justifies him.
>
> –St Augustine

that there was no way his merciful and loving Lord would be the one to shower all these catastrophes upon him and consequently he knew the enemy of the Lord was the one trying to damage his faith. Tearing his clothes is therefore not a sign of blasphemy, as some scholars believe, but rather a way of humbling himself before God. He wanted to be rid of all the possessions that remained with him, his clothes, thus leaving the enemy no means by which he could further test him. He wanted to strip down 'with' his enemy and he fell to the ground in humility and meekness before God; feeling that he is a sinner, and that his soul has fallen down to dust. His words that follow exhibit Job in all his wisdom and explore a deep philosophy regarding assets and their relationship with eternal life. "He said: Naked I came from my mother's womb, and naked shall I return there. The Lord gave, and the Lord has taken away; Blessed be the name of the Lord" (Job 1: 21). The Bible never mentions any praise expressed by Adam or Eve, when they were in paradise enjoying all those glorious gifts and blessings. But it did mention this short praise articulated by Job, that surpasses many others; a praise that brings pleasure to the heart of God, and the hearts of the heavenly creatures; a praise that will remain engraved, as though on a rock, for the generations to sing, and for mankind to find by it divine comfort along the generations. We would not have experienced such life of inner delight in the psalms if the prophet David had not been a man of torment; and we would not have sung the praise of the three saintly youth, if they were not cast in the fire. By saying what he said, Job proclaims his return to his origin; according to the words of the wise Solomon: "The dust will return to the earth as it was" (Ecclesiastes 12:7). Job acknowledges that he has lost nothing that was his own to claim; for everything he had, even his children, were God's, His gifts to him. Accordingly, upon recognizing this fact of life, Job did not sulk or complain, as we would most likely do, but instead he bowed his head to the ground in prayer, teaching us the truth behind the quote, "the shortest distance between a problem and its solution is the distance between your knees and the floor; the man who is able to kneel down before God, can stand up to anything!"

What the Fathers Say

If you thank God, He will lift up from you the cloud of sadness; and you will say together with Job: "The Lord gave, and the Lord has taken away; Blessed be the name of the Lord" (Job 1: 21).

– St. John Chrysostom

REFLECTION

How often do I think of my own short-comings and weaknesses instead of remembering God's love and mercy? Let's focus on God's strength, and not our inability

A PRAYER INSPIRED BY JOB

Amid affliction my soul gives You
thanks and praise.

Because my heart is lifted up to You;

It has no other place in this world.

Nor the world has a place in it.

Fill my heart with all Your divine peace.

Grant my soul rest from the trials of this world;

Allow not my attachment to
this world detach me from You,

"Naked I came, naked I shall return,

Blessed be Your Holy and Glorified Name."

Amen

CHAPTER 2

THE TRIAL CONTINUES

Job 2:1-3

For a second time, a chapter in Job opens up with a meeting between God, His angels and the devil. As we saw in chapter 1, the devil has no power to harm our possessions or us unless he is given permission from God. When we read this a second time and concentrate on what is being said, we discover just how powerless the devil really is without the chance, to the extent where he does not even utter a word unless God allows him. Both times he presents himself before God, it is God who questions him and asks, "From where do you come?" (Job 2:2) giving him authorization to speak. This is a good reminder of not only the weakness of the devil, but of the great power of God! Some times we can be tricked into thinking that God and the devil are in a fight and it's an equal battle. The book of Job serves to remind us that this is not the case and that God, through His mercy and grace, gives us also "dominion over serpents, scorpions and all the powers of the enemy" as we pray in the thanksgiving prayer each morning.

The devil responds to God's question by saying, "From going to and fro on the earth, and from walking back and forth on it," (Job 2:2) which is fascinating to read. Often, due to our limited knowledge on the devil, we believe that he exists in a prison underneath the earth as a red monster that has a large pointy tail and holds a trident, just as we see him portrayed in cartoons. This verse serves to correct those false ideas we have of him. It forces us to question: does the devil really walk on the earth? Walking alongside us throughout the day as we go to school and work and perform our daily routines? Yes, he does. And throughout the whole day he looks for sneaky ways to make us fall and curse God. This can be a scary thought for some of us, but what we can find comfort in is knowing that, just as the devil walks around us as a "roaring lion, seeking whom he may devour," (1 Peter 5:8) so too does our Lord walk with us, protecting us from the devil's evil schemes as it says in Deuteronomy 31:8, "He is the One who goes before you. He will be with you, He will not leave you nor forsake you; do not fear nor be dismayed." This is such a beautiful picture, that God stands before us fighting away the

What the Fathers Say

Why is he resuming the attack? What should we learn from this? Even if we fall a thousand times, Satan will keep on attacking us, he will not hesitate to go on fighting.

— St. John Chrysostom

Job's Three Friends

Eliphaz was a Temanite meaning he resided in an important town of Edom; Bildad was a Shuhite which meant that he was a direct descendant of Shuah, son of Abraham and Keturah; Zophar was a Naamathite which is a Gentile name designated to people who came from Naamah, a city in Canaan.

Job's Wife

Based on tradition, some Jews have strong reason to believe that Job's wife was actually Dinah the daughter of Jacob who was defiled by Shechem in Genesis 34

People, Places &Things

attacks of the enemy so that we will not be harmed. We will see the tools that the devil uses against us to try and make us stumble as we go on.

"Then the Lord said to Satan, 'Have you considered My servant Job, that there is none like him on the earth, a blameless and upright man, one who fears God and shuns evil. And still he holds fast to integrity, although you incited Me against him, to destroy him without cause'" (Job 2: 3)

Again, the Lord proudly showcases His "servant Job" before the enemy but this time He rubs the righteousness of Job in the face of the devil by saying, in essence, 'even though all his possessions were taken away; his livelihood was eliminated and his family was killed, his faith still did not fail. And though you thought his faith would stutter under your tricks, he still shunned you, you wicked one!' As we saw earlier, God gave us power over all the powers of the enemy and through the example of Job, we see the pride that God has in His children who resist evil; so much so, that He rubs it in Satan's face. This resistance of evil is a great quality to have as a Christian as it shows amazing resilience in the face of trials and something that God will commend us on. I like to think of this as a soccer player who, after being fouled several times by the opposition, still manages to get back up and score a goal, putting salt in the wounds of the opposition who tried so hard to keep him down. This draws our minds towards the verse that reads, "A righteous man may fall seven times and rise again." (Proverbs 24:16).

Job 2:4-6

Satan intended to crush Job's character by saying: "Skin for skin! Yes, all that a man has, he will give for his life'" (Job 2:4). He meant that man does not care for whatever losses, even if it comes to his own family including his children, as long as he personally is healthy, and nothing touches his skin. If his skin was to be touched then he would get frustrated and "curse God" (Job 2:5) as Satan thought he would. This thought is not surprising coming from Satan who, in his truest form, is a proud being who thinks of nothing but himself and he expects us as humans to do likewise. This pride to think that "how dare God allow me to be harmed" is satanic and is an idea that must exit our minds as quickly as it entered. The devil is naturally selfish, and wants us to only be preoccupied with our health, comfort, and the safety of our own bodies. The Lord, once again trusting in His servant Job and his judgment, gives the devil permission to touch his skin with the condition that he "spare his life" (Job 2:6). This expression "Spare his life" could be comprehended that the temptation should be only within limits, and not meant to destroy him. As we know, "God is faithful, He will not allow you to be tempted beyond what you are able, but with the temptation will also make the way of escape, that you may be able to bear it," (1 Cor. 10:13). This presumes that had God even thought that the

We can say that 'Job' was not struck without cause; for, without the temptations he went through, others would not get such an example of virtue and perseverance.

— St. Gregory the Great

Having found out that the righteous fighter has not softened off, Satan thought of using his wife; probably saying to himself: This man 'Job' could not be stronger than Adam. Although he is rich, yet he does not have 'the paradise ...

righteousness of His servant Job would falter, He still trusted that he would rise once more by making sure the devil "spared his life," He allowed for a way of escape if he were to fall. In other words, temptations are meant to reveal man's weakness; allowing him to be humble before God, and keeping him from being proud. However, if it surpasses the limit of man's endurance, he would probably end up falling into despair and depression, and his soul would perish because of loss of faith. On Earth, there is nothing visible to us which does not show one of two things; the wickedness of Man or the Glory of God. We will be made known of the weakness of man without God, or the power of man with God. God reveals His power most when we are powerless. He carried that cross, drenched in our sin to prove to us that He is powerful enough to carry us when we can't carry ourselves. That's the ultimate show of power! And that is what we are tested on daily, our ability to be resilient in the face of trials whilst always seeking the strength of God to carry us when our journey feels too tough.

Job 2:7-10

Once the devil was given permission, he did not hesitate to go and strike "Job with painful boils from the sole of his foot to the crown of his head," (Job 2:7) leaving no part of his body, besides his tongue, untouched or unharmed. It's easy to admire the diligence of the devil towards his work, that he would use all his vigor and effort to try and stifle us.

You can't deny his dedication to his work, but it places a stronger emphasis on St Paul's instruction to "put on the whole armor of God, that you may be able to stand against the wiles of the devil," (Ephesians 6:11), as without the security of God we will crumble under this ruthless and vigorous attack of the devil who shows no mercy to his prey.

What follows this attack for Job is the truest test of his faith in God and something that we, as Christians in today's society, face regularly. "Then his wife said to him, 'Do you still hold fast to your integrity? Curse God and die!'" (Job 2:9). How often do we hear things like this in our lives? When we are at school and people question why we have a cross around our necks only seeking to mock our Christianity to try and entice us into living their unrighteous lives. How many times do we hear the words "just one drink?" or how many times are we invited to places we don't feel comfortable, as children of God, going to? This is the equivalent to the question posed to Job by his wife. Each day we are given the opportunity to do one of two things: curse God with our wickedness or praise Him with our righteousness. Too often we choose to reject the statutes of God and curse Him, and a lot of the time we use our youth as an excuse to "have a little fun while we're young and be holy when we grow up." Ever heard that before? Hear the response of Job and engrave them into your heart as though it is the key to unlocking the joy of the Lord towards you;

What the Fathers Say

... of God'; Although he is righteous, yet he did not have the "tree of life"; Although he is pious, yet Adam enjoyed talking with God; And although he possesses a great number of beasts, Adam, on the other hand, had all the animals of the earth at his disposal. So, if I managed to deprive Adam of all that through his wife, this man 'Job' will not be able to stand against the attacks of his wife!

– Father Hesychius of Jerusalem

What the Fathers Say

We can say that 'Job' was not struck without cause; for, without the temptations he went through, others would not get such an example of virtue and perseverance.

– St. Gregory the Great

"You speak as one of the foolish women speaks. Shall we indeed accept good from God, and shall we not accept adversity? In all this Job did not sin with his lips," (Job 2:10). The wisdom of Job lies in his understanding of the nature of God that both the good and bad that is dealt to him from the hands of the Lord are for the sake of his Salvation. What I find extremely interesting is his use of the word 'we' even after his wife seemed to have ridiculed him. Why didn't Job simply say, "Shall I indeed accept good from God...?" Rather, Job chose to use a word that signified fellowship and unity because he understood the tricks of the devil, who seeks to cause divisions in the body of Christ. The enemy used to strike believers by dividing members of a household and still does to this day. He did this with Adam using his wife Eve; And with David, using his wife Michal, who mocked him. He even used the apostle Peter against his Master, the Lord Christ, when Christ was talking about crucifixion, he said to Him "Far be it from You, Lord; this will not happen to you. But He turned and said to Peter: Get behind Me, Satan; You are an offense to Me, for you are not mindful of the things of God, but the things of men" (Matthew 16: 22, 23). The righteous Job understood the ways of the Lord, that every thing He does, whether good or bad, is ultimately for the sake of his own salvation, and so just as Jesus did with Peter, Job rebuked his wife.

Job 2:11-13

Job's three friends, Eliphaz, Bildad and Zophar, upon seeing Job in all his suffering on the ground, "made an appointment together to come and mourn with him, and to comfort him," (Job 2:11). This is the beginning of a long dialogue that ensues over the majority of the remainder of the entire book. It is incredible to see the lesson on friendship given to us by his friends in this situation before the dialogue begins. Not only do they come to comfort him but it goes on to say, "they lifted their voices and wept...for they saw that his grief was very great," (Job 2: 12-13). This is the true love in fellowship that Paul speaks about when he says, "Rejoice with those who rejoice, and weep with those who weep," (Romans 12:15), that the emotions of my friend will directly reflect on me and I will be there to celebrate with them in times of joy and to comfort them in times of suffering.

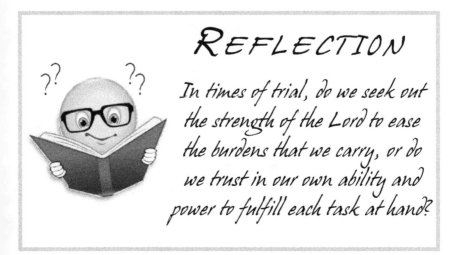

REFLECTION

In times of trial, do we seek out the strength of the Lord to ease the burdens that we carry, or do we trust in our own ability and power to fulfill each task at hand?

CHAPTER 3

THE BURDEN OF LOSS

Events

CHAPTER 3

As Job's friends sat around him comforting him with their presence and joining him in silence, "Job opened his mouth and cursed the day of his birth" (Job 3:1). This is a blatant contrast to his words of praise and glorification in the previous chapters. And although his friends surrounded him and tried to comfort him, most probably Job did not even feel their attendance, nor preoccupy himself with their company. Rather, he began to uncover the unpleasant emotions in the depths of his heart; and presented what is widely considered as the most powerful lamentation in the history of mankind; that bore an awful portrait of misery. The same Job, who only just prior to this moment had said, "shall we only accept good from the Lord and not accept the bad?" was now cursing the moment he was placed onto this earth for the entirety of chapter 3. What Job did that is a good example to all of us is what happened prior to the cursing of his birth, in that he maintained a long silence. In Lamentations 3 it says, "It is good for a man to bear the yoke in his youth. Let him sit alone and keep silent," (Lam 3:27-28). This silence is a time of contemplation on the matters and issues in our lives in order to understand the second part of this lamentation by Jeremiah that states, "because God has laid it on him" (Lam 3:28). Without this understanding that each burden we carry is the Lords form of correcting us on our path to spiritual perfection, there is always the danger and likelihood that we would fall into a state of depression. This chapter in Job is the beginning of his fall into that exact state as rather than seeing God's hand working in his life; Job instead chose to use this time of silence to think about all that he has lost and how fruitless his life had become. Whenever we sit in silence, what we are required to do is 'rise above ourselves'; to be meditating on the matters that concern God and His people; and not with what concerns our dignity and ourselves. Then, the Spirit of God would lift us up, as though to heaven, to hear the divine voice, and to discover the divine secrets, that would grant us the living hope. It is to understand in depth why it is that the Lord has allowed us to suffer and to essentially discover the truth in St Paul's words when he says, "Now if we are afflicted, it is for your consolation and salvation, which is effective for enduring the same sufferings which we also suffer. Or if we are comforted, it is for your consolation and salvation," (2 Cor. 1:6).

Stars

In the Holy Book, the term 'stars', is sometimes used to describe the righteousness of the saints, shining in the darkness of this life; And sometimes, to refer to the vain outer appearance of the hypocrites, who practice goodness for the sake of praise from men. If the doers of goodness were not stars, Paul would not say to his disciple: "In the midst of a crooked and perverse generation, among whom you shine as lights in the world" (Philippians 2: 15).

People, Places &Things

What the Fathers Say

Death of the righteous became rather like sleep, and even like life.

– St. Basil the Great

"And Job spoke and said..." (Job 3: 2)

After seven days of silence with his friends, Job is the first to open his mouth and speak openly regarding his demise. This goes to show two things: the first is the extent to which Job was suffering. His suffering and misery were so great that his friends are portrayed as horrified by their inability to utter a single word of comfort to their friend in his time of wretchedness. It's easy to read a story like this and not understand the magnitude of the happenings. However, when we read about the perspectives of other characters within the story, we begin to develop a complete picture of the tale and experience the entire range of emotions attached to it. This is what happens when we see the reaction of his friends in simply their lack of words upon seeing their suffering friend. It was such a great affliction that was thrust upon Job; no words could ease the burden. And that is the second thing we learn from their silence, that sometimes when we see someone in distress, it may be better and more comforting of us to say nothing at all rather than trying to construct a statement of reassurance for them. This is a hard thing to do as oftentimes we may face opposing reasons to maintaining silence. One of these reasons includes the awkwardness of quietness. It is sometimes "awkward" or "uncomfortable" for us to keep quiet when a friend has just gone through some kind of tribulation whether great or small. For instance, we have all experienced a friend getting yelled at by their parents and throughout the ordeal we find ourselves awkwardly fumbling about trying not to pay attention to what is going on. When the parent leaves the room, to try and eliminate the awkwardness of the episode, we try and make a joke or a comment, often making the situation even more uncomfortable than it was before. The second reason, and one that is influenced strongly by the devil, is pride. It is hard when someone close to us is sorrowful or in a great deal of agony to resist the urge to let our opinions or advice made known. Sometimes the advice is requested but if it is unwanted or not sufficient, then it could potentially serve to cause more misery to the person in need. If that is the consequence of our advice then it is probably because it was given out of pride. It was given because I felt the obligation to impart wisdom or knowledge even though I may never (most probably) experienced the things which he or she is suffering to know how to come through it. In this case, my lips should remain sealed like the friends of Job as it is probably more consoling to them for me to say nothing at all. If ever I feel the "need" to open my mouth for any reason other than love and care for my friend I should remember, "And if anyone thinks that he knows anything, he knows nothing yet as he ought to know." (1 Corinthians 8:2).

For considering that his birth was the beginning of all his misery, Job commits a major

> ## What the Fathers Say
>
> *Death is here praised and thanked; as it takes away some from evil; and frees others from their misery; Some would find in it a refuge from evil; and others, an obstacle in the way of deceit.*
>
> *– St. John Chrysostom*

What the Fathers Say

There is a contrition of heart, spiritual and beneficial, that touches the depths of the heart; And there is as well another sort of contrition, harmful and disturbing, that only leads to defeat (like despair).

– St. Mark the monk

fault against the goodness of the Lord. Instead of remembering his years of plenty, when God blessed him in an abundance that people can only pray fervently for, Job selected a wicked path of remembering only his wicked days, which were few, and subsequently cursed his entire existence. Draw your mind back to chapter 1, the beginning of his trial, when Job proclaimed the most beautiful blessing of the Lord, "Naked I came from my mother's womb and naked I shall return there. The Lord gave, and the Lord has taken away; BLESSED be the name of the Lord," (Job 1:21). Those words can be repeated for all eternity because of how sweet they are and yet this same man speaks in this chapter as though he never said those words at all, as though he no longer has the same defiance in his belief. Proving true the concept in the epistle of St James, "Out of the same mouth proceed blessing and cursing," (James 3:10). So what happened to Job? Where did this faithful and trusting Job disappear? How could a man who was celebrating the will of God now speak about the day of his birth and say, "May the stars of its morning be dark; May it look for light, but have none; And not see the dawning of the day" (Job 3: 9)?

Job began to stumble in his faith as his hope of the Lord's deliverance was fading as the time of trial went on. And we too fall into this trap of losing faith as time wears on. Waiting for a job interview that you hope will come but never does, pleading for healing of a sickness that you pray the Lord will deliver you from but never does, trying to fix a broken relationship where the crack keeps getting larger. At all times our faith must endure to the very end, and when all hope seems lost, instead of cursing like Job, we must obtain one thing that rebuilds our faith: COURAGE. Courage that, when it seems as though the deliverance of God will not come, we can say 'The Lord has delivered, does deliver, and will always deliver me.' As Rebecca Currington says in her book 'Everyday Blessings', "You never know where courage will pop up in your life, because you never know what you'll face that will require it. You can be sure, though, that God will give you courage when you need it. God is both your protector and strength. So be confident that whatever you face, you do not face it alone. You face today with resources both from your own soul and the spirit that dwells within you." So when times get tough, be faithful and trust in the perfect plan of God; and when times only seem to get tougher, find the courage to turn to God and say, "I know you still hold me."

What the Fathers Say

Man's perseverance produces hope; and the good hope glorifies man.

– Evagrius

REFLECTION

Do I help a friend in need because of my love for them or do I do it for some ulterior motive?

CHAPTERS 4-5

THE FIRST FRIEND SPEAKS

Events

CHAPTERS 4–5

Up until this point in the story of Job, it has simply been about Job suffering and the miserable state of sadness in which he had fallen into. As we know, his friends, who saw his suffering and heard his cry of desperation, accompanied him without opening their mouths. That is until now, when Eliphaz, who was the oldest of the three friends and most experienced, spoke up regarding his views on Job's current status. He begins a two-chapter accusation of Job and his lack of considered 'righteousness,' claiming that someone who was truly righteous would not have been dealt such evil. Eliphaz reinforces his argument by twice claiming to have heard the voice of God in a vision of some sort and uses this to strengthen his words. In all his apparent wisdom, Eliphaz proclaims to Job what he would have done had he been put in his shoes, again trying to accuse Job of wrong dealings with God. In spite of his false teachings, he then goes on to describe the truth of the acts of God but falls short again by failing to understand the ways of God in particular, His dealings with His servant Job throughout his trial. Each of Job's three friends possessed true faith in God, there is no denying that. However, each of them declared his faith in a different way just as we too are all given different gifts in the body of Christ.

Yet, Eliphaz was the most experienced and knowledgeable among them which gave him the courage to speak up first; even though he was unable to rightfully interpret God's work through the bare human mind and thinking. It is more appropriate for a man to appreciate that he is undeserving of interpreting God's plan and dealings with all of us, or to even grasp His mysteries.

"Then Eliphaz the Temanite answered and said..." (Job 4:1).

After Job spoke his words of pain and misery, Eliphaz thought it was a good time to respond to these words. Job, who probably spoke in a way that requested comfort and reassurance from his friends, did not receive either such things from Eliphaz who went on a poetic rant regarding Job's apparent righteousness. Eliphaz begins by asking, "If one attempts a word with you, will you become weary? But who can withhold himself from speaking? (Job 4:2), as though he is warning Job not to expect any comfort from him or his friends, whom he no doubt discussed with in the week prior to his opening account.

Eliphaz opens his account by commending Job saying, "Surely you have instructed many; And you have strengthened weak hands" (Job 4:3) and also saying, "Your words have upheld him who was stumbling, and you have strengthened the feeble knees" (Job 4:4) referring to the way Job preached and ministered to the weaker citizens of the town so faithfully, as though he were ministering to the angels. He does not take

What the Fathers Say

When you hear how the divine majesty is exalted above heavens; its glory is un-expressible; its beauty is un-describable; and its nature unapproachable; Do not despair to be able to see what you long to see. It is in your capacity; As within you, is the level by which you can realize the divine things. He, who created you, has granted you, at the same time, that amazing exaltation.

– St. Gregory of Nyssa

anything away from Job in that respect. In fact, Eliphaz provides us, by showing the good characteristics of Job, a living example of shepherding, and even for life of true faith; how every believer should care for his brother's life through love; without disregarding his care for his own salvation and that of his household.

No matter how much we try to shy away from these duties, as children of God we are called to do likewise and care for those around us. Sometimes this comes easy when we are ministering to our friends or family whom we already have love for, but we are called to also extend our sphere of care as much as we can, otherwise the words of the Lord might apply to us: "what reward will you have" (Matthew 5:46).

Notice how Eliphaz, when talking about the service of Job, speaks about his service towards the "weak hands," the one "who was stumbling," and the "feeble knees." He refers to those who are the lowest in society as those who were apart of Job's most significant of ministries. And so, we know now that it is not to those who we are comfortable being around that we are called to serve alone, rather, we are called to serve those who have no one to serve them. That means the homeless, the poor, the sick, the needy and all those who we so often pray for out loud without ever applying ourselves in helping them. More practically, we are asked to reach out to those who may have no friends, who may not be the most popular, who may be difficult to speak to. We can all identify these people and just as easily as we identify them, we ignore them. Not Job. Job was an honest servant who chose rather to serve these 'weak' members of society rather than live a life solely focused on himself and his family.

Still, Eliphaz follows these words of praise by mocking Job's change in fortune saying "But now it comes upon you, and you are weary; It touches you and you are troubled" (Job 4: 5). Eliphaz criticizes Job, suggesting that, when he is called to drink of the cup of suffering, he falls into ruins, becomes weary, and frightened. What Eliphaz is essentially condemning Job of wrongfully, is the sin of hypocrisy. It is as though he says to him: 'When you were wealthy and your life was full of blessing, you were a good preacher and it did not harm you to help others; but, falling into destitution, you ran out of goodness, and your weakness is exposed.' This is similar to the way in which Christ Himself was rebuked whilst He was on the cross as the scribes and elders mocked Him saying, "He saved others; Himself He cannot save," (Matthew 27:42).

That Jesus, who was the Son of God and lived a completely blameless life, also suffered and was rebuked in the same manner as Job. This really highlights the foolishness in Eliphaz's following statement, "Remember now, who ever perished being innocent? Or where were the upright ever cut

What the Fathers Say

Those who are fond of debating, attack the life of the righteous by two ways: Either confirming that what they say is wrong; Or that the truth they say, is not reflected on their own behavior; which was the way, the righteous 'Job' was rebuked by his friends, after they started by commending him. The wicked, so as not to appear as such, sometimes say about the righteous, the good things they are known to have, and are difficult to deny.

— St. Gregory the Great

off?" (Job 4: 7).

"May the Lord of love, to whom we pray, take away from our Spirits, every hate, bitterness, and anger, to grant us – through our binding to each other in a tight union, as different members of one body (Ephesians 4: 16) – To present to Him, by one accord, one mouth, and one Spirit, the praise of thanksgiving due to Him .

– St. John Chrysostom

REASONS FOR SUFFERING

Eliphaz being unaware of the behaviors of God, could not comprehend why God, in His great mercy, would allow a righteous man to suffer, and so he rashly concluded that Job was not a righteous man. God, however, allows suffering for four reasons, some of which Eliphaz was unmindful. The first of these reasons is for punishment, when there is no hope for restoration as God says in Jeremiah 30:15, "Why do you cry about your affliction? Your sorrow is incurable. Because of the multitude of your iniquities, Because your sins have increased, I have done these things to you."

The second reason is to bring a sinner to repentance. We know the story about how Jesus healed the lame man besides the pool of Bethsaida and says to him in John 5:14, "See, you have been made well. Sin no more LEST A WORSE THING COME UPON YOU," reminding him that it was his sin that caused him this great affliction and his repentance will save him from a much worse affliction; eternal death.

The third reason why God allows suffering is to prevent future sins. St Paul understood this concept of suffering for the prevention of sins, namely pride in his case as he exclaims in his second epistle to the Corinthians, "And lest I should be exalted above measure by the abundance of the revelations, a thorn in the flesh was given to me, a messenger of Satan to buffer me, lest I be exalted above measure," (2 Cor. 12:7).

The fourth and final reason is so "that the power of God might be made known," (John 9:3) as Christ tells His disciples when they question Him regarding the man who was born blind asking, "Rabbi, who sinned, this man or his parents, that he was born blind?" (John 9:2). When we acknowledge and understand these four reasons that God allows suffering in this world, we see that it is out of His mercy rather than His wrath that He allows us to suffer. Always seeking to return us from the error of our ways or keep us walking on an upright path.

ELIPHAZ CONTINUES

Eliphaz, seeking to justify his condemnation of Job, tells him about a vision he saw before he spoke up to him and says with descriptive and poetic language, "Then a spirit passed before my face; The hair on my body stood up" (Job 4: 15). It was most probably an angel sent by God, who came to minister to His word. The hair of his body stood up; as the heavenly creatures became a subject of horror to men since the fall of Adam; for fear that they may be carrying a painful message, never expecting good news.

However, Eliphaz using this vision to rebuke Job supports St Gregory's comments that the friends of Job, particularly Eliphaz, were nothing more than false teachers, who pretend to hear the hidden secrets of God in order to confuse the weak and to cast a "veil of reverence" over their preaching. It is important to remember this in our service. We should never approach someone whom we serve from a superior position but rather we should adhere to the word as it stands, "servant," and be humble in our dealings with people so that God may work through us. As we know, "God resists the proud, but gives grace to the humble" (James 4:6).

Thinking himself to be wiser and more righteous than his friend Job, Eliphaz rebukes the way Job dealt with his sufferings by exclaiming what he would have done had he gone through the misery Job suffered. "But as for me, I would seek God, And to God I would commit my cause" (Job 5:8).

This is indeed a righteous response to affliction; that I would turn to God in times of distress and hardship. How often do I turn to God when my heart is burdened or broken by a trial in my life? God is always reaching out to us, promising us a life of renewal and restoration. All He needs from us is to turn to Him and hand over all our concerns, trusting that He can and will rescue us from our difficulties. Let's rewind for a moment though, taking into consideration the words of Eliphaz. What was Job's immediate response to his trial? Remember those beautiful words of praise that he uttered before the Lord? "He said: Naked I came from my mother's womb, and naked shall I return there. The Lord gave, and the Lord has taken away; Blessed be the name of the Lord" (Job 1: 21).

Was his response not in alignment with the suggestions of Eliphaz? Eliphaz was correct in his thinking, but to question the actions of a blameless man, Job, was the cause of his downfall. This theme continues throughout the chapter as Eliphaz goes on to speak beautiful and TRUE words regarding the works of God mentioning that He "does great things, and unsearchable, marvelous things without number" (Job 5:9) without taking into consideration, even for a moment, whom these words are directed to. Every Christian seeking to live a life of righteousness should adhere to the words of Eliphaz, although, in this context his words were misguided. Not more so than when he says, "He sets on high those who are lowly, and

Eliphaz

There is mention of another 'Eliphaz' in the bible (Genesis 36:10). A son of Esau with Adah, daughter of Elon the Hittite. The first-born son of Eliphaz, Esau's son, was called Teman, who was also the first chief of Edom and who probably gave his name to the city of Teman, where the chiefs of Edom resided. Many believe this to be the same Eliphaz who was the friend of Job.

those who mourn are lifted to safety" (Job 5:11) ironically prophesying the redemption of Job in the process of accusing him. St Gregory again comments that the remarks of Eliphaz throughout the duration of chapter 5 would have been true, had they not been delivered against the patience and righteousness of so great a man as Job. Nevertheless, Eliphaz then speaks words of utter magnificence, pure beauty. Words that, had Job understood from early on, he would have not spiraled into such a great heap of desolation. "Behold, happy is the man whom God corrects; therefore do not despise the chastening of the Almighty. For He bruises, but He binds up; He wounds, but His hands make whole" (Job 5:17-18).

Imagine this image: you are lying in your own pile of grief. You are bruised, wounded, broken-hearted, afflicted and alone. You are inflicted with a great pain and you are unable to rise from this isolation. And then a Man, a Man so beautiful in appearance and personality that He immediately brings you peace and joy, walks towards you with outstretched arms and promises you that He can heal you, that He can save you from this barrenness. Would you take His offer? Or would you sit in your heap of humiliation? Whenever you are in a state of sadness or suffering picture this image. Envision the words Christ would say to you as you lie there in all your sorrow. "My beloved," He says, "I have come so that you may have joy. Reach out and take my hand so that we may be together again." And finally He tells you, "I can repair your shattered heart." Not bad for a carpenter.

REFLECTION

How do we respond to the tribulations we are dealt with? Do we consider the goodness and mercy of God in those times or do we prefer to blame Him for our suffering?

CHAPTERS 6-7

CHAPTERS 6-7

The Complaint of Job

In times when all hope seems lost and your eyes have run dry from your tears, it is common to seek consolation in the arms of your dear friends. Particularly now where we live in an age that our closest friends are considered to be our family, we can always rely on their words of reassurance and comfort. Job did not find any of these things in the words of his friends as Eliphaz harshly criticized him and judged him wrongfully. Job did not disagree with the words of his friend regarding the fact that all the punishments he suffered were granted to him by the permission of God, but "why" they had been granted was where there argument lied. Eliphaz argued that Job's suffering was a penalty for hidden sins that Job had not told them about but Job in these next two chapters argues against that and claims that, even if that were the case, his friends should have compassion on him rather than beat him down saying harshly at one point, "A despairing man should have the devotion of his friends, even though he forsakes the fear of the Almighty" (Job 6: 14). Fr. Tadros Yacoub Malaty comments on this situation exclaiming that Job was very much grieved and disappointed by the attitude of his friends, who tried to hint to him that God has become his enemy. What mostly hurt and confused him; was to be told that God whom he loved and worshipped, has brought on him all those disasters, and has put him under all those signs of His wrath; which led him to long for death to relieve him of his troubles. Had the friends of Job treated him and his emotions with gentle-kindness, as the Lord so often does, it may have served to strengthen his faith and trust in God throughout his pain. This is a lesson to us as servants, that when we are dealing with anyone among us who is suffering, we should be gentle and loving towards them, reminding them of the compassion of our God. In chapter 7, Job presents to us a living depiction of what is appropriate for the believer to do in the midst of his troubles, especially, as far as his relationship with his adversaries is concerned; or in his case, his friends. He did not neglect or ignore them, and he definitely did not disrespect them but rather, he talked to them intelligently, calmly, and truthfully. Yet, we see that every so often, he would turn his face to the side, raise his voice up to God and enter with Him into an honest prayer. Thus, chapter 7 came as a prayer from a heart tasting the bitterness

What the Fathers Say

"The salvation of Israel has been through the sea; and the salvation of the whole world is realized through the washing by the word of God"

-St. Cyril of Jerusalem

REFLECTION

How can we learn and remember that our bodies are temples for the Holy Spirit? boys should read the stories of the female saints and likewise, girls should do the same with the male saints.

What the Fathers Say

Who would be given the title "Scales", other than the 'Intercessor' between God and men, who came to weigh the worthiness of our life; bringing with Him both justice and compassion together?

– St. Gregory the Great

from his friends, resorting to God, his unique heavenly Friend, grantor of comfort and the savior of his soul. This is a characteristic we see in many of the Old Testament heroes. A heart that, when agonizing, turns to the Lord for relief. King David in all his psalms begins in a state of unease and pain but ends joyfully knowing that the Lord has heard his cries and will bring all things to pass peacefully as he says, "The Lord will perfect that which concerns me; Your mercy, O Lord, endures forever" (Psalm 138:8).

Job, realizing his unique sense of despair, begins chapter 6 complaining that, if even his friends could not understand, then no one would be able to understand the extent to which he was suffering saying, "Oh, that my grief were fully weighed, And my calamity laid with it on the scales!" (Job 6:2). Certainly Job was trying to use this to justify his actions and his behaviors and although he may have been proven wrong to be in such a state of sadness, knowing full well that God would deliver him, it was not for his friends to judge his actions. And by this we discover that the "scale" that Job speaks of is the Lord Christ Himself as He is the only One with the capacity to judge and condemn our actions and by the standards that He set alone we ought to follow. St Gregory the great reaffirms this idea of Christ being the scale as He "came to weigh the merit of our life, and brought down with Him both justice and loving-kindness together."

THE ARROWS OF THE ALMIGHTY

"For the arrows of the Almighty are within me; my spirit drinks in their poison; the terrors of God are arrayed against me" (Job 6: 4). Although he did not find any comfort in these words of his, Job speaks a wonderful thing about heaven and the army of God here. What are these "arrows of the Almighty" but God's arrows targeted at His saints to wound them with His divine love, that let them yearn for death so that they may confront Him and experience His love in the most perfect way in Heaven! Job did not see it as such but rather thought that these arrows, sent to harm him in the form of his calamities, were meant to injure his hope in God and so he would be unable to find comfort in raising his eyes up to Heaven where these afflictions were being brought down. The fathers believe that God the Father, out of His unconditional love for mankind, has aimed His most precious arrow – His Word – at the hearts of men, to wound them with the wounds of love, that their souls would cry out, saying: "I am lovesick" (Song of Solomon 2:5). In other translations this verse reads as: "I am wounded with love." Hence, God aims the arrows of His love at our hearts to grant them the wounds of love, together with gladness on an eternal level. Similarly, yet contrastingly, "fiery darts of the wicked one" (Ephesians 6:16) are aimed at the hearts of men to kill them, and to sentence them to an eternity of punishment.

Job 6:8-29

Following his attempts to justify his reaction to his trials, Job restates his desire that the Lord allow him to rest in death saying, "Oh, that I might have my request, that God would grant what I hope for" (Job 6: 8) (that being death). This is very similar to Jonah who, when his spirit was crushed, cried out saying, "Oh Lord, please take my life from me, for it is better for me to die than to live," (Jonah 4:3).

This is a feeling we all suffer from at times when our hearts and souls feel broken. It is important however, to follow the lead of Job who, although making a foolish request of God, never cursed Him or His word even unto death rather saying, "For I have not concealed the words of the Holy One," (Job 6:10). If we look at Jobs situation, isn't it funny how the same problems we have to deal with today, existed back then and were suffered by someone as righteous as Job? What was his dilemma? Why did he request death at this point? Why not when he lost all his possessions initially? It is because he felt alone! Although his friends stood beside him physically; they stood against him spiritually.

"My brothers have dealt deceitfully," (Job 6:15) he says, shocked at their lack of understanding. Job expects nothing less than love and kindness from his friends, as we all do in our times of brokenness, yet he receives neither. He knows not to expect from his friends consolation in the form of gifts or even protection from the attacks of the devil (Job 6:22-23) and he is accepting of rebuking if it is found to be just (Job 6:24) but he doesn't understand why they would be so "forceful" with him in the vulnerable state he is in (Job 6:25-27). Sometimes we too can feel as though even our friends are "out to get us" or "don't care about our feelings," and this can be really damaging to our souls and make us feel this unbearable pain we call "loneliness." This is the beginning of the division of Job and his friends as Job stays true to himself and maintains his loyalty to God despite their false accusations "...my righteousness still stands!" (Job 6:29).

Job 7

Jobs' prayer in chapter 7 is something that, while directed entirely to God from the brokenness of his heart, portrays a man who sees the world as a miserable place to live. "Are not his (mans') days also like the days of a hired man?" (Job 7:1), he says likening life to a working day for a 'servant' or 'slave' in some translations. He goes on to say, in equally negative tone, "Like a servant who earnestly desires the shade," (Job 7:2) suggesting that we are constantly seeking something more in life.

Job's understanding that man is a "servant" on earth is not wrong, however he sees it from a very pessimistic point of view. We are in actual fact servants on earth

- servants for Christ. As St Paul instructs us in Colossians 3:23, "And whatever you do, do it heartily, as to the Lord and not to men." When we understand this then we will feel the "sweetness" of laboring for God rather than this pain and agony that Job feels. Again, this feeling is a consequence of his calamities as suggested by his statement "I have been allotted months of futility," (Job 7:3). Because of his negative view of this life of service, and his lack of understanding that his service should be only towards God, Job thus feels that there is only one way to end his days of hardship – death. He speaks about this desire using very scary language saying, "So that my soul chooses strangling and death rather than this body" (Job 7: 15). This is such a huge contrast to someone like David who holds his peace in times of suffering and distress as he says, "I was mute with silence; I held my peace" (Psalm 39: 2). David teaches us the beautiful lesson of silence and peace when we feel moved to wrath whereas Job loses his peace with God, asking Him to relieve him of

People, Places &Things

Tema

A center of trade routes in northwest Arabia (6:19)

Sheba

A center of trade in southwest Arabia (6:19).

Till I swallow

"Till I swallow" (7:19) is a common proverbial term used to mean "a short time."

his life completely.

The meekness of Job shines through in the end though as he asks God modestly, "Have I sinned? What have I done to You, O Watcher of men? Why have You set me as your target, So that I am a burden to myself?" (Job 7: 20). The term "Watcher of men" here is highly important to look at in the grand scheme of Jobs' situation. God is an ever-present figure in our lives, watching over us through the good times and the bad. So is Job suggesting that God has stopped looking over him? Perhaps. Little does he understand God's amazing plan for his life. God put him through this fire so that he may be refined just as we often run into tough times in life only to realize that it was God testing our faith and endurance. God will not test our hope in Him more than we can withstand. As we will see in the story of Job, when our hope has reached its limit, God shows up!

REFLECTION

Do the friends around me encourage me and fill me with hope or am I constantly unhappy when I am with them?

CHAPTER 8

BILDAD ACCUSES JOB

"Then Bildad the Shuhite answered and said..." (Job 8:1)

By Bildad responding to the words of Job, rather than Eliphaz who triggered those words, we see that the friends were in agreement regarding their stance to Job's sufferings – that he was justly punished for his sins. More than that, Bildad comments that "if your sons have sinned against Him, He has cast them away for their transgressions," (Job 8:4) suggesting to Job that the death of his children was a consequence of their sins. This suggestion would for sure anger Job all the more! Job used to present burnt offerings on behalf of his children (Job 1:5) fearing that they might stray from the path of God and so it would have pained him all the more to even consider these words of Bildad. Bildad, who claims to understand the justice of God in this whole chapter, ironically misjudges this situation entirely. Bildad gives us a lesson on how NOT to deal with our friends when they are in need of our support. St John Chrysostom believes that it was an extremely aggressive way in which Bildad presented his argument towards Job. If he were a little more patient and understanding, he would recognize that what Job had said was a normal reaction to the terrible sufferings and temptations he is passing through.

After accusing Job of his response to his calamities, Bildad makes another

CHAPTER 8

funny suggestion to Job saying, "If you would earnestly seek God and make your supplication to the Almighty," (Job 8:5). Is Bildad really telling Job how it is he should pray? No doubt there is a great power in prayer, particularly when it comes from a broken heart and as Father Aphrahat says "prayer is an inner encounter of the pure heart with the Holy God; A talk of the heart, which would not please God, unless it is pure." However, is this not what Job had been doing all his life? Persisting in prayer with God from the early hours of the day throughout the day (Job 1:5)? So while Bildad makes a reasonable suggestion, he makes it in a rash manner, forgetting or not acknowledging whom it is he speaks to. He goes on to question the purity and uprightness of Job (Job 8:6) and claims that if he were, then God would make him great once more (Job 8:7). Bildad will soon come to eat his words when he sees the end that God has prepared for Job, proving that he is truly pure and upright. This is in like manner to how God deals with each of us. If we maintain our purity before God, then He will work His hand in our life in an amazing way no matter what trials we may suffer. If we can take one thing from the words of Bildad it's this: "Though your beginning was small, yet your latter end would increase abundantly," (Job 8:7). Though we may suffer and be persecuted, if we would just remain upright before God, He will deliver us and make us great.

What the Fathers Say

We should discern between these types of people: those whom it is befitting to love; those with whom we should bear, and those of whom we should be aware; the shepherd to be loved; the hired hand to bear with; and the thief to be aware of.
– St. Augustine

The devil is used to imitating the things concerning God; he sets false messengers to oppose the true ones; and he even takes the form of an angel to deceive men.
– Theodoret, Bishop of Coresh

What the Fathers Say

The soul always thrives by this joy; with it, it becomes happy; and by it, it ascends to heaven. Like the body, it has its spiritual food.

– St. Anthony the Great

While Eliphaz proposed that if Job was a righteous man then nothing would have occurred to him, Bildad openly and aggressively accuses Job of evil and hypocrisy. "Can the papyrus grow without a marsh? Can the reeds flourish without water?" (Job 8:11) he says comparing Job to these things that reveal hypocrisy. And although his words regarding hypocrisy are true beyond doubt, he directs them to the wrong person. It's actually funny, when you consider his words between Job 8: 8-19, you discover that they speak more of Bildad himself in all his foolishness rather than Job. Ponder these words. Bildad who believes there is no hope for Job to regain all that he has also says, "The hope of the hypocrite shall perish," (Job 8:13). Bildad who is confident that Job is impure and wicked also says, "Whose confidence shall be cut off," (Job 8:14). And Bildad who, along with his friends, represent to Job where he places in foundations in terms of trust and support also says, "His roots wrap around the rock heap," (Job 8:17) not knowing that he in fact symbolizes that rock heap for Job.

People, Places &Things

Bildad

Is a Babylonian name that means 'Old Friendship.' Bildad was a Shuhite being a descendant of Shuah, the son of Abraham and Keturah (Gen 25:1), whose family lived in the deserts of Arabia, or a resident of the district.

Despite the foolishness of his words, Bildad goes on to say something rather beautiful regarding the upright man (though he didn't direct it to Job). "Behold, God will not cast away the blameless, nor will He uphold the evildoers," (Job 8:20). These words will prove to be true for both Job and his friends. We will see how God restores the "blameless" Job and puts to shame the "evildoers" in the form of his friends. I can't imagine the pain suffered by Job as a result of the brutal accusations from his friends. But if one thing is true it is this: "The mouths of the righteous will be filled with laughing, and their hearts will be filled with eternal joy, when the tears of their journey are consummated." (St. Gregory the Great). Meaning that no matter how painful or heartbreaking our trials may be, if we fix our gaze upon God and uphold our righteousness before Him, He will turn our tears into laughing, our sadness into dancing and our trials into a triumph.

REFLECTION

Do I seek God with all my heart and mind or do I only go to Him when I am in need of something?

Chapters 9-10

THE DEPRESSION OF JOB

CHAPTERS 9-10

Job chapters 9 and 10 both begin to reveal more about the thoughts running through the mind of Job and how those thoughts are translated in his prayers. Job doesn't disregard Bildad's argument against him, but in his meekness he rather searches honestly for a solution to the problems Bildad presented to him. He doesn't accuse him of being too harsh with him or criticize him for his blatant hypocrisy, choosing to remain humble instead saying, "Truly I know it is so," acknowledging and accepting the cruel words of Bildad and then humbly questioning him asking, "But how can a man be righteous before God?" (Job 9:2). So, not only does Job not rebuke the words of Bildad, but he also seeks his guidance on the matter he has presented to him, that is, righteousness before God. It's actually a fair question in the context of human weakness, that in the sight of God, who is all holy and perfect, then how can us as humans in all our weakness be made righteous before Him? There are people in the bible who were granted the honor of being called "righteous before God." The most famous of these are Zacharias and Elizabeth. So what made them righteous before God? How can we too be granted this honor? It says of them "they were both righteous before God, walking in all the commandments and ordinances of the Lord blameless," (Luke 1:6). To then obtain this "righteousness before God" we must take His commandments seriously and abide by His word in our lives.

Job 9:3-32

Acknowledging the vastly superior mind of God, Job questions how it would be possible to challenge or even discuss His exalted works face to face with Him. It's difficult for Job to comprehend the possibility of this because of His knowledge of the wisdom of God saying, "If one wished to contend with Him, He could not answer Him one time out of a thousand" (Job 9:3). And so because of this, Job feels that it would prevail nothing to struggle or resist with God as he insists, "God is wise in heart and mighty in strength. Who has hardened himself against Him and prospered?" (Job 9:4). This is contrary to the dealings of God in the bible who grants blessings to those who struggle with Him including Jacob who "wrestled with Him until the breaking of day," (Genesis 32:24) until God blessed him. Also the story of the woman who wearied Christ until she had her prayer answered because of her persistence with Him. Job feels in contrast to this because amidst all his sufferings, all he senses is that God is being too hard on him. True that He "removes the mountains" (Job 9:5), "shakes the earth," (Job 9:6), "commands the sun," (Job 9:7) and "spreads out the Heavens," (Job 9:8) as Job recognizes, but he still goes on to say that "God will not withdraw His anger," (Job 9:13) accepting the authority of God and forgetting His great mercy on His creation. He says it in a very harsh way, even questioning God's

> **What the Fathers Say**
>
> Whoever seeks peace, seeks Christ, being Himself Peace.
>
> – St. Basil the Great

desire to hear his voice speaking, "If I called and He answered me, I would not believe He was listening to my voice," (Job 9:16). Again this is not a true representation of God who, in all His compassion for mankind, would never choose to ignore the voice of His children especially in the midst of their anguish. Even King Ahab, who was known as the worst King to rule over Israel, had his voice heard by God when God proclaimed, "See how Ahab has humbled himself before Me? Because he has humbled himself before Me, I will not bring calamity in his days." (1 Kings 21:29).

Despite His lack of faith in the mercy of his Lord, Job still confirms his own righteousness by saying: "Although I am blameless, I have no concern for myself, I despise my own life" (Job 9:21); namely, that he holds onto to his righteousness, even at the expense of his own life. He refuses to die in wickedness. However, because he has made this assessment of his spirituality, he then questions the judgment of God assuming that, "It is all one thing; therefore I say, 'He destroys the blameless and the wicked," (Job 9:22). But is that really

People, Places &Things

Darkness

Darkness' was a part of the common understanding of the afterlife amongst Old Testament believers.

Uz

Uz was a land near Midian. Midian is the place Moses dwelt for 40 years before returning to Egypt to free the Hebrew captives from under the slavery of Pharaoh.

the case? Of course not! If God punished the righteous with the wicked then there would be no motivation to gain righteousness. Again, this opposes the meditations of David the king who said in his psalms, "Therefore the ungodly shall not stand in the judgment, Nor sinners in the congregation of the righteous. For the LORD knows the way of the righteous, but the way of the ungodly shall perish." (Psalm 1:5-6). The only way Job feels he can restore his relationship with God would be to meet Him and speak to Him face to face as we often do. Thinking that for our lives to change or for our hearts to be transformed then we must have a direct interaction with God Himself. But does Job have any way of reaching Him? It is difficult for him to ponder this thought, "For He is not a man, as I am, that I may answer Him, and that we should go to court together," (Job 9:32). This is the point in the story of Job where Job loses all hope of reconciling with God, or at least what he feels needs reconciling. In his complaints against God, he speaks about Him as though He is absent, as though He is no longer present in the midst of his troubles. This follows the theme of chapter 9 where all of Job's thoughts and feelings are in opposition to the teachings and promises of God who says in Isaiah, "Fear not for I am with you; Be not dismayed for I am your God. I will strengthen you, Yes, I will help you, I will uphold you with My righteous right hand," (Isaiah 41:10).

What the Fathers Say

We have the right to be there in the presence of God in heaven, we, who have kept the lesson while being on earth; then went up to heaven to be in the love of God the Father, whom we knew while on earth; And because God, the holy Word has done everything, taught, and still teaches us everything, and training us on all good things.

– St. Clement of Alexandria

Job 10:1-22

What the Fathers Say

Whoever tells about his sins in disgust; should speak out in the bitterness of his soul; for the bitterness itself to be a punishment for the attempts of his tongue to justify his conscience. But, we must put into consideration that this brings on a kind of security against the pains of regret; lifting them up to confront with greater confidence the examination of the heavenly Judge.

— St. Gregory the Great

Job is evidence that even the most righteous children of God can forget Him in times of trouble and disregard His merciful nature. Once you forget the mercy of God in your life, you run the risk of falling into a deep depression, thinking that your sin can be too overwhelming and that God wants nothing to do with you in all your wickedness, or you may be suffering from a personal issue and you've lost hope in the saving hand of God. This was the state that Job found himself in saying, "My soul loathes my life... I will speak in the bitterness of my life," (Job 10:1). Particularly as teens we are prone to speaking words like these, words like "oh I hate my life," or "I wish God would just end my life." Maybe it's a failed exam, a divorce in the family, a broken relationship or anything that brings us down; it is comforting to know that even the righteous have these same thoughts that even someone as righteous as Job would curse his life and lose hope. But nevertheless, we MUST remember God in our afflictions. We must not blame Him for our sufferings like Job did exclaiming, "Does it seem good to You that You should oppress, that You should despise the work of Your hands?" (Job 10:3). We must not feel these things towards God but rather always remember that we are His handiwork and that He will not forsake us. Job does the first part of this remembering, "You have made me like clay," (Job 10:9) acknowledging that he is the handiwork of

God but then saying, "You hunt me like a fierce lion," (Job 10:16) assuming that because of his pain, the fact that he is the handiwork of God means nothing to Him and He has not only forsaken him but will hunt him and destroy him. This is a depression in its darkest sense of the word. How dark and painful are the words of Job? How often do we too allow the sufferings in our life take us to a depression of such a dark extent? We only suffer this same dark depression when we forget the mercy of God and the infinite love He has for us, His children. Let us never repeat the dark words of Job in our times of despair who says, "A land as dark as darkness itself, As the shadow of death without any order, where even the light is like darkness." (Job 10:22).

REFLECTION

Am I wearing a mask, pretending to be someone I am not? Do I do that in front of God also?

A PRAYER INSPIRED BY JOB

O Lord, When I am troubled, remind me
that You are my Comfort.

When I am anxious, remind me
that You are my Peace.

When I am suffering, remind me
that You are my Relief.

When I am broken, remind me
that You are my Potter.

And Lord, when all hope seems lost, when I find
myself so overwhelmed in the depths of my sin,
remind me that You alone are my Salvation.

Amen

CHAPTER 11

KNOWING GOD

You have probably heard the phrase, "to put salt in a wound." Well, in this chapter, Zophar is the salt. He comes across as a very simple, caring fellow, but just like Bildad and Eliphaz, he was arrogant. Not only that, although he speaks with sound logic and truth, he lacked fellowship with his brother Job during his time of suffering and so he added salt to the wounds of his friend. Unfortunately, that theme will repeat itself time and time again with the friends of Job throughout the entire book, which is why people tend to struggle through this book in the Bible. So, rather than only focusing on the negative mentality of Zophar, let us examine his words and take a positive message from them.

On God, Zophar states wonderful things. He says that He does not stumble in His judgment (11:5-6), that His perfection is immeasurable (11:7-9), His authority is infinite (11:10) and that His knowledge is complete (11:11-12). Where Zophar erred is in his analysis of Job – saying that he was "full of talk" (11:2) and that he spoke "empty words" (11:3). It's extremely difficult to understand how someone who has such a profound understanding of the nature of God, can only manage to see the 'corruption' in a man of God. It comes down to the disparity between knowing about God, and actually knowing God. It is easy to know about God. I attend

CHAPTER 11

bible studies, I read up on commentaries, I study theology, I read spiritual books, etc. If I do all these things, then it's true, I may know all about God. But there is only one way to truly know God: that is, through prayer.

How can you really know someone if you do not communicate with them? There is a funny analogy by Fr Daniel Fanous who once compared this to a guy trying to get to know a girl. First the guy speaks to her close friends (the bible) and enquires about what she's like in social situations. Then he approaches her parents (the church) and asks them what she is like at home. He also speaks to her colleagues (the saints) to find out what it's like to work with her. Can he then turn around and say "I love this girl" or more so "I know her"? Of course not. He can't possible know her if he never took the time to speak to her. He knows about her sure, but he doesn't know her in anyway.

What's funny still, is that prayer is the advice Zophar gave to Job. He says to him, "If

What the Fathers Say

Silence for God's sake is good; and talking for God's sake is good as well.

– Abba Poemen

Naamah

Naamah is a descendant of Cain mentioned in Gen 4:22. She was the only mentioned daughter of Lamech and Zillah and their youngest child. Her descendants, like Zophar, are known as Naamathites.

Zophar

Zophar is a Hebrew name that means 'Rising Early' or 'Crown.'

People, Places &Things

you would prepare your heart, and stretch out your hands toward Him, then surely you could lift up your face without spot" (11:13, 15).

It is crucial that we ask ourselves today: do I know God, or do I just know about Him? If I know Him, then let me speak about Him freely. Otherwise, as it should have been in Zophar's case, it is better to keep silent.

REFLECTION

Am I always the first to speak, or do I take a moment to listen first?

CHAPTERS 12-14

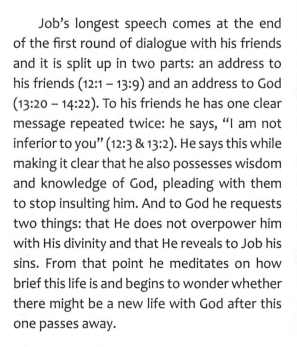

APPROACHING THE CREATOR

Job's longest speech comes at the end of the first round of dialogue with his friends and it is split up in two parts: an address to his friends (12:1 – 13:9) and an address to God (13:20 – 14:22). To his friends he has one clear message repeated twice: he says, "I am not inferior to you" (12:3 & 13:2). He says this while making it clear that he also possesses wisdom and knowledge of God, pleading with them to stop insulting him. And to God he requests two things: that He does not overpower him with His divinity and that He reveals to Job his sins. From that point he meditates on how brief this life is and begins to wonder whether there might be a new life with God after this one passes away.

Job tells his friends that the 'knowledge' which they imparted on him is known by all of nature, it is common knowledge shared by all of creation. He says, "asks the beasts of the field" (12:7) like Balaam's donkey who talked, and "ask the birds of the air" (12:7) who neither sow nor reap nor gather into barns (Mt 6:26), and "the fish of the sea will explain it to you," (12:8) like the large fish which swallowed Jonah. By whose orders did these things occur? Or in the words of Job, "who among all these does not know that the hand of the Lord has done this?" (12:9). And so, Job exhorts his friends to question their words to him. And he follows this up with a warning: "Oh that you would be silent, and it would be your wisdom!" (13:5). Sometimes the best thing to do when faced with a question is to say, 'I don't know.' Sometimes it is wisest to remain silent. Men have the hardest time with this. When asked for directions, even if they don't have a clue, men will give directions.

I DON'T KNOW

Imagine driving on the road and someone pulls up next to you and asks for directions to a supermarket. You have no idea where it is but you guess, thinking 'I'm never going to see this person again anyway.' Two weeks later you meet the same person outside a Café when they begin yelling profanities at you for getting them lost. It's funny, but this is the scenario Job presents to his friends, except it's not a random on the street, it's God! "Will it be well with you when He searches you out?" (13:9) he asks them. 'Will God find your words to be true? To be righteous? Or will He rebuke you for speaking lies?' It is a scary thought!

What the Fathers Say

Who could be justified in the eyes of God, or could boast of his righteousness and the purity of his heart, if an infant of one day is not considered pure of sin!

– St. Ambrose

People, Places &Things

onds of kings

Bonds of kings' (12:18) e the bands with which ngs used to fasten their bes. They are led away ptive in only a 'belt,' herwise known as a oincloth.'

the Hebrew word as it is used here indicates that God will 'preserve' Job's sins with plaster until judgment day.

Sealed up

'Sealed up' (14:17): in the courts in those times, any charges against a criminal were kept in a sealed bag so that none would be lost; all would be held against him when he faced the judge.

over

'cover' as it is entioned in 14:17 is not hat we think it means. ther, the meaning of

Which is why I need to be careful with what I say and when I say it. When a group of youth from St Mark's church, Sydney visited Kenya, the first thing they were taught was, "when you preach, go in pairs. One person speaks, and the other person prays for the speaker." It's a reminder that our words can have such an enormous effect on the lives of those around us and so it is vital that we pray each day for the Lord to guide our tongues to speak only words that are pleasing to Him.

Job then goes on to ask God for two favours. First he says, "withdraw Your hand far from me" (13:21) in fear that he will become afraid of God's deity. Job believes strongly that the Lord is overwhelming him and so he pleads for 'mercy,' that God's hand would leave him. But is that true? No. It is actually the presence of God's hand that has allowed Job to survive his turmoil and not the cause of it. We should never pray for God's hand to depart from our lives. We should rather pray that His hand is in everything we do and touch.

MY INIQUITIES

The second thing Job asks God is that He reveals to him his iniquities saying, "Make me know my transgression and my sin" (13:23). This is a beautiful prayer request, one that we should adopt in our spiritual lives. We can often be blinded to our own faults and so we must seek God to bring to knowledge our shortcomings so we can make the necessary changes. I once bought a cheap smart watch from a local tech shop, when one day, the extra features stopped working and all I could see was the time. Usually this wouldn't bother me but I kept thinking, 'without all these extra features, it's just a normal watch.' So, I purposed to fix it. I tried playing with the knobs and buttons for a few days myself but to no avail. So, I went back to the shop to speak to the man who sold it to me. He tried for a few minutes but couldn't fix it either. He then told me to come back that afternoon when his dad, the maker of the watches in the shop, would be back, so I did. That afternoon I returned and within minutes of handing my watch to the owner, it was fixed. The reason is simple. The maker of the watch knew how to fix it because, he could see the problem. He knew how the watch was supposed to function and all the little things within it that allowed it to function and so, when things weren't how they were supposed to be, he recognized it. The watch could not recognize its own problem, I couldn't recognize it, not even the seller could recognize it, only the creator. And it is a similar thing with God. Sometimes only He can reveal to us our deepest iniquities, because He created us to function a certain way and when we veer off that way, He may be the only one to recognize that.

Following this, Job makes one final request of God, that He "look away from him that he may rest, till like a hired man he

What the Fathers Say

The further away the hired man is from the end of his day's work, the further away would be the wage for his labor. That is why every saint in this life, would grieve more when they see that the day of their departure from this life is far away. They would grieve that they are still far from the eternal blessing.

— St. Gregory the Great

finishes his day" (14:6). Job is pleading with God that He allows him to work on his own without persistently 'punishing' him so he can at least experience the satisfaction of an employee going about his business. It can be a common misconception that, if I serve God, then I am exempt of any suffering. This is not true. God allows us to suffer for our growth. But He doesn't want us to grow alone, He wants us to learn to suffer with Him so that in turn, we may grow with Him. Ask yourself: am I like Job who asks the Lord to 'look away' in times of suffering? Or am I like King David who says to the Lord, 'Look on my affliction and my pain, And forgive all my sins' (Ps 25:18)?

REFLECTION

God's mercies are new every morning. Do I ask Him every day to have compassion on me and forgive me for my sins?

CHAPTER 15

JOB FOR TEENS

ELIPHAZ SPEAKS A SECOND TIME

Chapter 15 marks the second round of conversations between Job and his three friends, once more beginning with Eliphaz. Fr. Tadros Yacoub Malaty summarises the first round of conversations as follows:

Eliphaz: God is pure
Job: Yet He is disturbing me.

Bildad: God rules and establishes things well
Job: Yet He does not allow me to stand before Him.

Zophar: God is the whole Wisdom and no one is wise like God
Job: I still wish to appeal my case to Him.

TRUE HUMILITY

The second round of discussions begins much more viciously with Eliphaz accusing Job of 'faking' his righteousness and wisdom saying, "Should the wise answer with empty knowledge, and fill their bellies with the hot east wind? Should they argue with unprofitable talk, or in words with which they can do no good?'" (Job 15: 1-3) arguing that the wisdom and knowledge of Job was all a trick so that he could seem righteous before men. It's not uncommon for us to fall into this sort of trap, acting 'holy' or 'humble' before other people so that we can seem righteous but, when we go home, we never take the time to pray to God, read our bibles or eat from the spiritual food we've been given on a

Events

CHAPTER 15

daily basis. Particularly with humility we tend to make the mistake of thinking that I must be miserable to be humble and that I need to walk around with my head down so that other people would see me as being humble. C.S Lewis describes true humility however as, "not thinking less of yourself, but thinking of yourself less." Which means, not thinking of myself in a negative way but rather, spending less time thinking selfishly and looking out for the interests of others instead. I guess we can apply this same rule with true and un-deceitful wisdom as well, spending less time speaking extravagant words about deep topics to make myself seem wise but rather, spending more time speaking to Wisdom Himself, that is Christ, who gives wisdom freely to all who ask for it. All of this is not to say that Job fell into this trick of self-righteousness and deceitful wisdom, but just to show that it is something to be wary about.

These allegations made against Job by Eliphaz mimic the constant attacks against

What the Fathers Say

He who cries out to God with the voice of true humility and genuine faith, is a lamb; whereas he, who utters blasphemies against the truth, and bears animosity against God, is a wolf!

– St. John Chrysostom

ast wind

he 'east wind' brought rritation because of its xtreme heat.

atness

atness' was an old stament word used to scribe wealth and earthly ccess.

Himself

The use of 'himself' in this context means 'the lower abdomen,' or one's innermost being. This may be a pun to suggest that Job's words are full of hot air and come from his gut, not from his reasoning.

People, Places & Things

What the Fathers Say

It is well said: "Heaven itself is not pure in His sight"; As before the particular knowledge of God. Even those preaching purity could not be found pure; as testified by St. John, saying: "If we say that we have no sin, we deceive ourselves, and the truth is not in us" (1 John 1: 8). So now, if no one among the saints is unchangeable, and if heaven itself is not pure in the sight of God, who can claim that he practices true righteousness?!

– St. Gregory the Great

the Church that we receive even up until today. Often times, whether we are at School, University or anywhere else outside the Church, we are accused of following certain things that the Church ascribes to all its followers that have no need. Sometimes it's the Church itself, other times it's the Bible and more often it's the traditions of the Church. These are things that Christ Himself instituted for us and the Church has held firmly onto all of them in all its abundant wisdom. The same way Job's hypocritical friends attack this righteous man, heretics continue to attack the Church and its teachings.

Eliphaz goes on to say to Job, "What is man that he could be pure? And he, who is born of a woman, that he could be righteous?" (Job 15: 14). This is not incorrect, it's very true that before God no man can be found pure and in His sight no one can be considered righteous due to the corruption of human nature. And this statement reiterates the words of Job himself who said, "Who can bring a clean thing out of an unclean?" (Job 14: 4). Therefore, while we strive for righteousness and perfection, we can never say that we have attained it when we stand before God as Eliphaz mentioned. However, Eliphaz, in all his manipulative ways, says this in a way to make Job out to seem wicked by applying this fact to Job, but not to himself. So, he who accused Job of self-righteousness unconsciously falls into the exact same trap. It teaches us the lesson that we should not be so quick to judge, because we are all weak sinners who are inclined to falling into sin.

JUDGE NOT

There were once two men who worked at the same company. Let's call them Luke and John. Both of them were required to come into work at 8am to complete their respective tasks for the day. For almost 2 weeks, Luke would run late by about 15 minutes every day and this would aggravate John, who began complaining about Luke's constant lateness. Due to his persistent complaining, their boss had no option but to let Luke go and fire him. About a month later, John's wife fell down the stairs and had to be taken to the hospital. John called in to work begging his boss to pardon him that day, as he knew he would be late. When he arrived at the hospital the doctors asked John and his wife if it was okay to place his wife in the same room as a little girl who had Leukemia, as there were no other available rooms. John and his wife happily agreed. When they entered the room, John saw Luke sitting by the bed of his youngest daughter, the little girl with Leukemia. It was in that moment that John realized why Luke was late every single day, because he was visiting his sick little girl. Crying, John fell at the feet of Luke and begged for his forgiveness, realizing how huge a mistake he made in being so quick to judge Luke.

Rather than putting someone down for their weakness, we should raise them up so

What the Fathers Say

We often said that the righteous 'Job' bears a symbol of the holy Church; and that his friends bear the likeness of the heretics, who pretend to defend the Lord, find chances to say foolish things, utter vile words against the good people; and everything the believers think offend them, and counted as words in the wind!

–St. Gregory the Great

that when we fall, God will look at us with the same compassion and raise us up also. Just as John wished for his boss to excuse him for coming late to work, he should also have excused Luke for his continual lateness. In the same way we pray each day in the Our Father, "Forgive us our trespasses as we forgive those who trespass against us."

REFLECTION

Do I make excuses for others? What do I often consume my life with? Am I careful with the things I watch and listen to?

CHAPTERS 16-17

CHOOSING YOUR FRIENDS

Events

CHAPTERS 16–17

After hearing the words of Eliphaz, we see Job becoming more and more agitated by the treatment of his friends towards him. He condemns them for their stubbornness in accusing him and reproaches them for being "Miserable comforters," (Job 16:2). Job causes his friends to think about the concept of the roles being reversed, if they were suffering and he was there to comfort them. He taught them a lesson in friendship when he says that if that were the case, "I would strengthen you with my mouth, and the comfort of my lips would relieve your grief," (Job 16:5). God grants us the gift of friendships in our lives for this very purpose, to comfort one another and encourage one another on our spiritual journeys. As it says in Ecclesiastes 4:9-10, "Two are better than one, because they have good reward for their labour. For if they fall, one will lift up his companion. But woe to him who is alone when he falls, for he has no one to help him up." The world is becoming a darker and darker place and there are so many people around us now who are falling into dark pits of depression, some of whom consider taking their own lives. We need to be wary about the way in which we speak to one another, as one harsh word could cause a lot of damage to someone we may care about. More than that, we need to be careful and think very wisely when it comes to choosing our friends. Ask yourself: are the 'friends' around me now raising me up spiritually and enjoyable to hang around? Or do I constantly find myself miserable in their company and struggling spiritually? If so, then I need to seriously reconsider their role in my life. Maybe, however, I'm the problem and I'm not allowing my friends to enjoy experiencing a spiritual environment when we hang out together. If I want good friends, I must be a good friend.

A SYMBOL OF THE SUFFERING CHRIST

The remainder of chapter 16 bares many resemblances to Lamentations chapter 3, which speaks about the sufferings of Jesus Christ from a prophetic first person view. Many lines are similar including, "You have made desolate all my company," (16:7), "He has set me up for His target," (16:12) and "My friends scorn me," (16:20). More than that, there are direct references to the sufferings of Christ such as, "They strike me reproachfully on the cheek, they gather together against me," (16:10), "He pours out my gall on the ground," (16:13), and "Oh that one might plead for a man with God," (16:21) showing Christ's role as the mediator between God and man through His passion. All of this highlights the deep agony that Job endured by making his suffering a likeness of the passion of Christ. Job becomes a symbol of the suffering Christ.

"My spirit is broken, My days are extinguished, The graves are ready for me" (Job 17: 1). Job begins chapter 17 as he ended

What the Fathers Say

It is the Lord Christ, although He never sinned by thought nor through deeds, Yet He became in bitterness by His passion; Who, set free by resurrection; became, by His ascension to heaven, on the right side of the Father, as our Guarantor.

– St. Gregory the Great

What the Fathers Say

A friend who rebukes another in secret, is a wise physician; but he who does it publicly before the eyes of many, is actually a reviler. A righteous man follows the lead of the Lord in not chastening man for the sake of avenging his evil, but of reforming him for the benefit of others.

– St. Isaac the Syrian

chapter 16, amidst his agony and misery. Reaching such a miserable state of mind, Job considers himself as good as dead. In the midst of his bitterness, he feels that his spirit has been broken, the light of his days have been overcome by darkness and extinguished; and lying on such a heap of trash, he counts himself already in the depths of the grave. This is a result of Job feeling as though he has suffered a form of injustice, being punished for a sin he didn't commit and accused by his friends of something he didn't do. And although he knows himself to be blameless before God, he still understands God's role as a Redeemer and wishes that He would plead his cause for him saying, "Now, put down a pledge for me with Yourself," (Job 17:3). It is a natural human reaction that we seek after witnesses or someone to provide evidence of our goodness when we have been unfairly punished. Whether that is by our parents, our teachers or any one of the sorts.

HAVING CONVICTION

The thing Job lacked most was conviction in his faith and hope in God. He knew that God was a Redeemer who looked favourably upon those who followed after Him wholeheartedly and yet he still says, "As for my hope, who can see it? Will they go down to the gates of Sheol? Shall we have rest together in the dust?" (Job 17:16), abandoning all hope of the restoration of God. As Christians we must hold onto our faith with the utmost conviction, believing that God has the capacity to do more than our minds can fathom, and to save us even when we feel as though we are in the depths of the grave like Job. Fr. Antony Paul in his article entitled 'Do you really think for yourself', inspires this concept by stating, "Ask yourself if you are truly bold enough to 'be who you are' and 'believe what you believe'. It does take courage to be different, it really does, and the only way to have the courage to stand out, is to know and believe that you are right with utmost conviction." It was this conviction in their faith that led all the disciples, except one, to be martyred for the sake of Christ, knowing and believing entirely that Christ would raise them and bring them into His eternal Paradise. Their faith was in the Cross and its power to redeem, but their conviction was proven in their deaths, placing all their hope in the Salvation of Christ. We also, should never be ashamed of our faith, never be ashamed to tell someone you went to church or that you are a Christian. Show some conviction in your Christianity and Christ will not deny you before His Father in Heaven.

What the Fathers Say

Finally, Let all my hope be in You. Let my treasure be in Your heavens. For there is no place more secure.

– Fr. Tadros Malaty

Sheol

When the Hebrew scriptures were translated into Greek in ancient Alexandria around 200BC, the word "Hades" (the Greek underworld) was substituted for Sheol.

People, Places &Things

St Kyriacou was a young 3-year-old boy who had only barely begun to speak, when he and his mother were brought before the Emperor to face persecution for being Christians. The Christians at that time were being killed for not worshipping the false gods and Kyriacou and his mother were two that were captured and told to do just that. The options that lay before them were: bow down to the fake gods and be saved, or confess to being Christians and be killed. Kyriacou, in spite of his young age, knew of the eternal life after death and the hope of restoration if He confessed Christ. So with great courage and conviction, Kyriacou cried with a loud voice, "I AM A CHRISTIAN." He and his mother were martyred for the sake of Christ and restored to the Heavenly Kingdom.

Let us never lose hope in the restoration of God, even when we feel as if we have fallen into a dark pit in our lives. The light of Christ is in us and it is that light that will be our shimmering hope in times of darkness.

REFLECTION

Do I speak to God as a Friend? Am I as honest with Him as I am with the friends around me? Do I have conviction and clarity in all that I do?

A PRAYER INSPIRED BY JOB

God is the one who lifts me up,

As only a true friend should,

And God is the one who was lifted up,

For me on that piece of wood.

For my sake He bled and bruised

And suffered on that road,

So for my Lord, my God and Friend,

I'll help carry that load.

In times of distress, anxiety or fear,

And times of desperate need,

I know I can look up to God,

Because He is a friend indeed.

CHAPTER 18

A PORTRAIT OF THE WICKED

It is now Bildad's turn to speak for a second time and, just like Eliphaz, the second time he speaks against Job is more cruel and harsh than the first time. The first time Bildad spoke up, he began mentioning the destiny of the wicked, those who stray from the commandments of God. On this second occasion, he doesn't add anything new but he gives a more holistic view of this destiny, which Fr. Tadros Malaty describes as, "A Gloomy Portrait of Destruction." Bildad provides this view that he believes applies to Job by saying of the wicked:

"The light of the wicked indeed goes out and the flame of his fire does not shine..." (18:5)

"The steps of his strength are shortened..." (18:7)

"He is cast into a net by his own feet and he walks into a snare. The net takes him by the heel and a snare lays hold of him." (18:8-9)

"Terrors frighten him on every side..." (18:11)

"His strength is starved and destruction is ready at his side." (18:12)

"He is driven from light into darkness and chased out of the world." (18:18)

He concludes this frightening portrait of the destination of the wicked by saying,

Events

CHAPTER 18

"Surely such are the dwellings of the wicked, and this is the place of him who does not know God," (18:21). Although Bildad showed a huge misjudgment of character by believing this was the destiny of Job, considering him to be wicked, he still presents a very true and terrifying account of the destination of the wicked.

"This is the place of him who does not know God..." (Job 18:21)

What does it mean for me to know God? At the end of time, Christ will say to us one of two things: if we choose to prepare ourselves and avoid the ways of the wicked then He will say, "Come, you blessed of My Father, inherit the kingdom prepared for you from the foundation of the world." (Matthew 25:34). He has prepared a place for us, we now have to prepare ourselves to inherit this place by persevering against the tricks of the enemy just as Job did. If we do, let us then expect to hear these joyful words from the mouth of our Lord. If not, then we will hear Him say, "I never knew you, depart from Me." (Matthew 7:23).

How can Christ say He never knew me? It's almost contradictory to everything He says to us in the bible. He says that He knew me from before I was born and that He knows the number of hairs on our head. He knows everything about me, everything I've done,

> ## What the Fathers Say
>
> *Do not be in the company of the adversaries; lest the legion of devils dwell in your house. Beware of the envious; because he is an incarnate devil.*
>
> *– St. John of Dalyatha*

What the
Fathers Say

*Satan never
aims his arrows
in daylight;
lest they would
be seen; as
everything done
in light, are
proclaimed by
light.*

– St. Jerome

everything I've said, everything I will do and say, how can He then come and say that He never knew me? In the language of the bible, the word, "know" means to have an intimate relationship with someone, generally a physical one. Which is why it says that St Mary "never knew" Joseph and never had any sort of physical relationship with him, but rather that she remained a virgin her entire life. So when Christ tells us that He never knew us what He's really saying is, "you never took the time to have an intimate relationship with Me. You never made the effort to make Me a familiar part of your day. You never wanted to know Me. How can you say you love Me if you never knew Me?"

It's just like going home to your parents to tell them you found "the one." Imagine this is how the conversation went:

You: "Mum, dad, I found the one of my dreams. I love them so much."

Parents: "Oh, congratulations, we're so happy for you. What's their name?"

You: "Uhh, not too sure, think it might start with a D."

People, Places &Things

Book of poetry

The book of Job is the longest ancient Hebrew poem ever known to have been composed. There was much difficulty throughout history in translating this book because of its unusual language and style.

Firstborn of death

'Firstborn of death' was a phrase used to describe death in its most complete, most formidable spiritual form.

Parents: "Okaaay, well what do they do?"

You: "Maybe studying, unless they graduated then they're working. Not sure though."

Parents: "Hmm. Well do you know what they look like?

You: "Yeah of course, they have hair... umm two eyes I think... but I love them."

Can we honestly say we love that person when we know absolutely nothing about them? The same goes with God, to tell God I love Him, and to show people that I love God, I need to get to know Him. I need to know Him in an intimate way by spending time at His feet in prayer and bible reading. So, we must spend our time on earth getting to know Christ in order to avoid this path of the wicked that Bildad describes.

REFLECTION

Do I set aside time each day for silence, prayer and the opportunity to grow and come closer to God?

CHAPTER 19

WHERE DOES MY HOPE LIE?

After Bildad accuses Job of going down the path of wickedness, Job presents himself as a broken man, pleading with his friends to have pity on him in his lonely state. The words of his friends seem to have a damaging effect on Job as he yells the cry of a defeated man saying, "How long will you torment my soul, and break me in pieces with your words?" (Job 19:2). We see Job slowly breaking, complaining that everyone is turning against him including his "brothers and acquaintances," (19:13) his "relatives and close friends," (19:14) those who "dwell in his house," (19:15) his "servant," (19:16) his "wife and his children," (19:17) and even his "close friends," (19:19) referring to the mistreatment he has been receiving from Eliphaz, Bildad and Zophar.

MY REDEEMER LIVES

Job feels that all these people in his life have betrayed him because God has made an enemy out of him. "He has fenced up my way, so that I cannot pass; He has set darkness in my path. He has stripped me of my glory, and taken the crown from my head. He breaks me down on every side, and I am gone," (Job 19:8-10). He feels as though everything going wrong in his life is a result of God turning His back on him and leaving him alone. He begs crying, "Have pity on me, have pity on me, O you my friends," (Job 19:21) in the midst of his isolation. But this is not in the nature of our God, to leave us alone and broken. Even when the whole world turns it's back on us, God is with us. Even if the whole world fights against us, God will fight for us. And even if the whole world hates and mocks us, God will still love us. The glory of God shines most through those who are broken, because so much of them has been carved away to make room for more of Him. We see this happen with Job in this chapter. Just at the edge of losing all hope, he speaks and says these beautiful prophetic words, "For I know that my Redeemer lives, And He shall stand at last on the earth; and after my skin is destroyed, this I know, that in my flesh I shall see God," (Job 19:25-26) prophesying about the coming resurrection of the Lord and his own subsequent resurrection after death. When all hope seemed lost, Job looks towards the resurrection and rediscovers his courage in God. In the center of his despair, Job looks towards the anticipation of the risen Lord. It's a lesson to us that after every cross we bear there is the knowledge and hope of a resurrection.

There is a story of an Olympic runner who won the gold medal in the 100-meter sprint at

What the Fathers Say

"I know that He is eternal, He who saves me on earth, setting up my skin that would endure all these things" (verse 25). That is why 'Job' says: "Oh, that my words are written (for the coming generations)"; As after passion, they will experience resurrection. It is positive that the body which receives passion will rise again.
– Father Hesychius of Jerusalem

People, Places & Things

atriachal societies

Patriarchal societies, the relationship between embers of the same ibe was very strong. ach member had a sponsibility toward every her member within their vn tribe.

Skin of my teeth

"Skin of my teeth" (19:20) is a metaphor meaning by the thinnest of margins.

'Redeemer' was a title for God used by the Hebrews of the Old Testament as being Israel's deliverer from the bondage in Egypt.

What the Fathers Say

"And I shall rise again on the last day on earth" (19:25). That is because the resurrection proclaimed by the Lord Christ in His Person, He will also, one day, grant to us. For which He has given us an advance payment that the members of His body would follow in the glory of their Head (Christ). Our Redeemer has gone through death, that we should not fear death. He has revealed resurrection that we should have a steadfast hope that we shall resurrect as well.
– St. John Chrysostom

the Olympics. While she was on the podium singing her national anthem, she burst out in tears. Overwhelmed she fell to her knees while her nation sang for her in the crowd. Asked after what it was that brought her to tears, she replied saying this: "I began training 4 years ago after the agony of losing in the last Olympics. Each year, I suffered a major injury that I was told I couldn't come back from. Each year I recovered and continued training day after day. Three months before the competition my dad died from cancer and I became so emotionally drained that I couldn't train. But just as I did before, I got back up and kept going, kept striving, because I knew what lay waiting for me at that finish line. Every time I fell, I got back up. So when I broke out in tears, all that went through my mind was how much I suffered, how much I struggled, how much I agonized and how, through all my heartache and pain, it was all worth it at the end."

There is a gold medal in Heaven waiting for each of us who struggle for the Kingdom here on earth and sometimes Christ needs to break us before He can mold us into something better. We first have to die with Him before we can rise with Him and this story of the Olympian's struggle is epitomized by Micah 7:8: "Do not rejoice over me, my enemy; when I fall, I will arise; when I sit in darkness, the Lord will be a light to me."

Don't ever fear or worry that God has left you or abandoned you. God is always with you, even in the darkness, training you for a podium place finish.

What the Fathers Say

Be sure to keep the purity and peace of your heart, to be able to behold the Lord your God.

– St. Ephram the Syrian

REFLECTION

What is my ultimate goal in life?

CHAPTER 20

JOB FOR TEENS

JOB IS MOCKED BY ZOPHAR

Zophar, so he doesn't feel left out, joins Bildad and Eliphaz in accusing Job for a second time and AGAIN, his second accusation is more ruthless than the first. The only reason he opened his mouth in the first place was because Job's words made him so angry that he couldn't resist responding as we see him say, "Therefore my anxious thoughts make me answer," (20:2). What follows is a very harsh attack on Job and once more on his apparent 'wickedness' (a theme that is beginning to drag on a little with his friends) saying things like "the triumphing of the wicked is short," (20:5) and "He swallows down riches and vomits them up again," (20:15). What could Job possibly have said that made Zophar so cruel against him? Didn't Job just talk about the hope of the Resurrection, Heaven and Salvation? Yes, and it is for exactly that reason that Zophar was angry. He believed Job to be a wicked man and that the only reason he spoke about those wonderful heavenly things was because he wanted them to believe that he was righteous. Zophar thinks Job is wrong to speak joyfully because of his sin, and tells him to be quiet and miserable so that God can forgive him his evil deeds.

How did Zophar miss the point of Job's prophetic speech so badly? How did he not also feel the hope of the Salvation that is to come? Because he wasn't listening. He didn't want to hear the voice of Job. He already

Events

CHAPTER 20

decided in his mind that Job was a bad man and so everything that came out of his mouth was just 'trash' and not worth listening to. This is exactly like the Pharisees, who after deciding in their hearts that Jesus wasn't a good man, weren't able to see Him as God. No matter how many sick people He healed, or blind people He gave sight to, or even lame people whom He gave the ability to walk; they did not see Him as the Messiah. In John chapter 5, Christ healed a certain man on the Sabbath who had an infirmity for 38 years. He had no ability to walk until Jesus told him to "Rise, take up your bed and walk," (John 5:8) and he was made well. Rather than glorify God for the great miracle they saw before their eyes, the Pharisees commented and said to the man who was healed, "It is the Sabbath; it is not lawful for you to carry your bed," (John 5:10). That much hate they had for Jesus that they chose to see bad in all the good that He did. They were blind to His goodness and deaf

What the Fathers Say

Anger would make tongues loose. Speech with no control would lead to ridicules, reviles false accusations, and violent confrontations.

– St. Basil the Great

Milk and Honey

Many scholars would agree that Israel adopted features of Canaanite theology and worship in the writing. Therefore, is of little surprise to find allusions to Astarte (fertility goddess) buried the bible; or that the language itself – the original Hebrew – reveals her fertile beauty in the image of the Promised Land as "flowing with milk and honey." Thus 'milk and honey' became synonymous with 'freedom' and 'prosperity' to the Israelites of the Old Testament.

People, Places &Things

to His teachings. This is the same way that Zophar was deaf to the joyful and hopeful words of Job. We should learn to listen rather than speak, for the one who listens learns more than the one who speaks.

What the Fathers Say

Those who prosper in the pleasures of this world would perish in the power of God. They prosper up to a moment, and then eternally perish. They prosper in unreal goods, and perish in real tortures.

– St. Augustine

REFLECTION

How quickly do I turn to anger to deal with my problems with my family and friends?

CHAPTER 21

JOB'S GENTLE RESPONSE TO REBUKE

Job, beginning to feel extremely outnumbered and surrounded, responds to Zophar in a very polite and gentle way. He begins his response saying, 'Listen carefully to my speech, and let this be your consolation" (21: 2). Job uses the language of fellowship and love to appeal his cause to his friends. How often do we respond to mockery with the same wisdom? Or do we tend to yell, scream and shout to prove that we are right whenever we find ourselves in an argument? It's an all too common practice today; 'the one who yells loudest wins.'

Job's overarching argument in this chapter revolves around the prosperity of the wicked saying, 'Why do the wicked live and become old, yes, become mighty in power?" (21:7). He is trying to make them understand that his suffering is evidence that he is not wicked by claiming that the wicked are successful whereas he is in a state of misery and despair. "They send forth their little ones like a flock, and their children dance. They sing to the tambourine and harp, and rejoice to the sound of the flute" (21: 12), he continues. It's something we feel oftentimes when we see people outside of the church who are successful in all aspects of their lives and all we can do is wonder, 'why?' 'How come?' 'I am good, I go to church, I pray and read my bible every day and yet, I am no where near as successful as this guy who has no relationship with God whatsoever.' Can we really say, this guy is happy? Can we truly say the wicked that are successful in the world are happy? The answer is yes, they are. Happiness is just dependent on happenings, if things around me are going well then I am happy. This happiness, which is temporary, can be found in the pleasures of this world. But, it is not joy. Joy is not happiness. Joy is a fruit of the Spirit that comes when you spend time in the presence of God, absorbing his goodness. It comes when you forsake the treasures of this world and lay up for yourselves treasures in Heaven knowing that there you will find everlasting joy. Joy is not temporary, it is eternal. When you look at the faces of the 21 Libyan martyrs, those men who were awaiting persecution with the knowledge that in only a few moments they would be united with their Lord and Saviour Jesus Christ, what do you see? Joy. Peace.

It is our duty then as Christians to never be disheartened when we see the happiness of others in the midst of our sufferings. We should never feel as though God has betrayed us, or that His mercy has abandoned us. Rather, we should feel joy knowing that we have been counted worthy to suffer trials

What the Fathers Say

He says, "(I beg you) to bear with me", showing humility to those who are swallowed by pride against him; in order to provoke them to consider the teaching of the saving truth. The saints in the fold of the Church, are ready, not only to teach what is right, but also to endure what would be practiced against them, and would not mind being ridiculed.
- St. Gregory the Great

Tambourine

The tambourine was an instrument used by the Israelites in times of rejoicing, like Miriam the prophetess following the exodus.

Harp

The harp was used during feasts held by royalty or in the chambers of kings to soothe them like David who played the harp for King Saul.

People, Places &Things

What the Fathers Say

Paul says that the main point is not that he and his fellow apostles would suffer; as that is something common to all; But it is rather, that they would suffer without despair or anger; and on the contrary, while being filled with joy. By this, they would confirm that the evil that dwell on them would turn into good.
– St. John Chrysostom

and tribulations for the sake of Christ, for the sake of everlasting joy. If we find ourselves surrounded by our enemies or those who seek to mock us and put us down like Job's friends, we need to remember to hold our peace and trust in the deliverance of God. In that we find our joy. Christ Himself instructed us to be joyful during these times when He taught the beatitudes saying, "Blessed are you when they revile and persecute you, and say all kinds of evil against you falsely for My sake. Rejoice and be exceedingly glad, for great is your reward in Heaven," (Matthew 5:12).

REFLECTION

Am I an observer or a participant in the liturgy and other services of the church?

CHAPTER 22

CHAPTER 22

CAN MAN PROFIT GOD?

This chapter marks the beginning of the third round of debates between Job and his friends. What needs to be noted however is that Zophar does not partake in this round of arguments but only Eliphaz and Bildad. Eliphaz again initiates the accusations against Job although; we see in this chapter that he is slightly more subdued in his allegations. He begins by begging the question, "Can man be profitable to God?" (22:2). It may be that we in our lives have asked this question or pondered this thought. When I serve in the house of God and feel that I am helping to build His kingdom here on earth, surely I make myself profitable to God? Right? Yes and no. It is true that all of Heaven and God Himself rejoices when the work of the Lord is being done here on earth. To say that it profits God is farfetched though. We can not add to God in all His glory and He in His majesty does not need us to accomplish His work. Can He not simply work through someone else in order to complete the tasks He sets out for us to do? Fr Tadros Yacoub Malaty says, "Man in his weakness, and with his limitations, could not be of any benefit to God, who is the whole perfection, and to whom nothing would be added. Would a candle be of any benefit to the sun? Or would a drop of water add anything to the ocean?" Simply put, it is more profitable for me to serve God than it is to Him. When I praise Him, serve Him, worship

Him, love Him and live a life solely devoted to Him, I am the one who benefits, not Him.

Many of the church fathers make mention of the truth of Eliphaz's words regarding the Lord's response to our repentance yet, he delivers this message in a way that attacks Job for specific sins which he believes he has committed in his 'wickedness,' saying things such as:

"Is not your wickedness great, and your iniquity without end?" (22: 5)

"You have not given the weary water to drink, and you have withheld bread from the hungry" (22: 7)

"You have sent widows away empty-handed, And the arms of the fatherless you have crushed" (22: 9)

Because of these apparent iniquities of Job, Eliphaz suggests to him that, "snares are all around you, and sudden fear troubles you," (22:10). It was for this reason that Eliphaz felt the need to advise Job on returning to God and the gifts that come from repenting of our sins. He begins his counsel by instructing, "now acquaint yourself with Him... Receive, please, instruction from His mouth, and lay up His words in your heart" (22:21,23). When someone lives a life of addiction to something, whether it be drugs, alcohol or any other type of addiction, they go through something called 'rehab' in order to overcome their addiction. In these rehab

> ## What the Fathers Say
>
> He is in no need for our services, the way masters need of their servants. Our works would return to us for our own benefit; according to the words of the Psalmist: "My goodness is nothing apart from You" (Psalm 16: 2). Tell me: Would it be of any benefit to God if I am righteous, Or would it do Him any harm if I am wicked? His nature is incorruptible; He would never be harmed; and is above any suffering.
>
> – St. John Chrysostom

What the
Fathers Say

It is a sin for man to instruct someone better than himself; like what the heretics do; on the assumption that what they think in their minds is coming from the mouth of God.

— St. Gregory the Great

centers, they interact with counselors who guide them and instruct them as to what they should do in order to escape from their habits. The difference between someone who overcomes and someone who falls back into their old ways when they leave the rehab center will come down to who was willing to humble themselves and heed the instructions given to them by their counselors. The same goes for our spiritual lives. We all tend to fall into wicked habits, some which hold us captive for what feels like a lifetime. Those who 'receive instruction from the mouth of God,' and 'lay up His words in our hearts,' are the ones who will be able to break the chains of sin that oppress them. The Bible is filled with the promises of deliverance from the mouth of God Himself, and yet every single day we fail to claim these promises, and for this reason we continue to allow ourselves to fall under the weight of our sin. We must learn to 'acquaint ourselves with the Lord,' by turning back to Him in repentance and claiming His promise to deliver us from the

People, Places &Things

Pledge

In Holy Scripture the term pledge [promise] may denote either the gifts of the Holy Spirit or the confession of sin. Thus, pledge is taken as the gift of the Holy Spirit, such as where it is said by St. Paul, "and given us the Spirit in our hearts." (2 Corinth 1:22). For we receive a pledge for this, that w[...] may have an assuranc[...] of the promise that is made to us. And so th[...] gift of the Holy Spirit called a pledge, becar[...] through this [Spirit] [...] soul is strengthened t[...] assuredness of the in[...] hope.

imprisonment to our wickedness. It is then that we can say the joyful words that Eliphaz spoke saying, "'Exaltation will come!' Then He will save the humble person," (22:29).

REFLECTION

Who am I accountable to? Do I seek counsel and guidance from my spiritual father often?

CHAPTERS 23-24

CHAPTERS 23–24

The silence of God in Job's anguish

As I sit there completing the last few questions on my exam, I look ahead of me to the front of the class and see my teacher, watching and waiting. Counting down the minutes until she has to call time on the exam. All the questions I answered confidently, she knows; those that were answered hesitantly or unanswered all together, she also knows. Yet, she continues to sit, in silence. Not saying a word. It is this image with which we must see the Lord in the story of Job. As his patience and perseverance is tested, God, the examiner, watches on patiently in silence, to see if Job will pass this test. He knows each step he will take, both the right and the wrong, but time has not yet been called on this particular test, so He stays silent. Job forgets this. He forgets that the Lord is an ever-present figure in our lives saying, "Oh, that I knew where I might find Him, That I might come to His seat" (23:3) proposing that the Lord had somehow abandoned him and had all of a sudden become "absent." An echo of these words are cried out in the book of Song of Songs, "Have you seen the one I love?" (Song 3: 3). In spite of this silence, Job holds fast to the fact that he has done no wrong and when the Lord does apparently 'return,' He will renew him as he says, "But He knows the way that I take; When He has tested me, I shall come forth as gold" (23:10). Just as gold is molded and refined in the fire, so too are we polished by the fire of trials and tribulations just as Job said. In all of this, we should never lose doubt in the presence of God and continue to hold fast to our righteousness when He does finally decide to call time on our testing. When we are in the midst of suffering, He is there, only silent.

The time of our testing will be officially concluded at the Day of Judgment when the Lord will come and evaluate how we spent our time on earth. Whether we were loyal to Him in times of temptation or whether we succumbed to the traps of the wicked one. Whether we rose up in repentance after we've fallen into sin, or whether we played with sin with no hint of regret. Job questions whether he will ever see this day saying, "Since times are not hidden from the Almighty, Why do those who know Him see not His days?" (24:1). Looking forward to the Day of Judgment, Job is full of reverence and fear towards God,

dge

judge is a person who is authority to make wful decisions. Biblically eaking, the king was ways the supreme judge, cause his was the timate ruling authority. is on that basis, per d Testament writers, t God is the judge of

the world. Job, along with other Old Testament characters (including Moses, David and Isaiah to name a few), saw God as the absolute Judge, capable of judging even those who were given the authority to judge here on Earth.

People, Places &Things

What the Fathers Say

Do not hasten to rebuke anyone; but remember all the time, your departure from this body; and never forget the day of eternal judgment. If you do this, you will sin no more. Our spiritual fathers told us that seclusion is a school to remind us of death, and to teach us how to escape from everything concerning the flesh.

– St. Anthony the Great

at the prospect of encountering Him who is beyond time itself. Just because we feel as though this day is far off, we still live with the reality of its imminent coming so that we may not turn away from the Lord. God hid the day of His coming from humans in the hope that all would forsake their evil ways, lest that day would come all of a sudden over them. It is on this day that the Lord will conclude His testing and there will only be one of two results for each of us: pass or fail. The wicked will go one way, and the Lord will take the righteous with Him. The wicked will be rejected and abolished as Job says, "As drought and heat consume the snow waters, so the grave consumes those who have sinned" (24: 19). The righteous will be lifted up by the strong hand of God as he also says, "But God drags away the mighty by His power; He gives them security, and they rely on it; Yet His eyes are on their ways" (24:22,23). These are facts of life. God will come, He will judge and for those that lived lives dedicated to Him, they will also rise with Him. These words cannot

People, Places &Things

The Author of Job

The book of Job is one of the only books in the Bible whose author is unknown. Yet, his words spoken are written in great detail, leading scholars to believe that it is possible Job himself wrote the book.

be debated as Job proclaims, "Now if it is not so, who will prove me a liar, and make my speech worth nothing?" (24:25). These words were spoken in an effort to put an end to the debating between his friends and himself.

REFLECTION

Am I patient when I am waiting for God to answer my prayers or do I give up on prayer easily?

Chapters 25-27

CHAPTERS 25-27

BILDAD AND JOB EXCHANGE QUESTIONS

The thing that frustrated Job's friends most about Job, was his unwillingness to admit to his wickedness and instead stubbornly cling to his claims to be righteous and blameless before God. Bildad tries to cleverly convince Job that no man can be deemed righteous before the Almighty questioning, "Is there any number to His armies? Upon whom does His light not rise? How then can man be righteous before God?" (25:3-4). To an extent this may seem true. When I contrast my weakness to the glory of God almighty, what am I but dust? I am not worthy to stand before the Lord in my corruption and wickedness. To say that righteousness before Him is unachievable though, is a mockery to His grace. Christ calls us all to "Be perfect just as your Heavenly Father is perfect," (Matthew 5:48). On top of this it is said that, "With man this is impossible, but with God all things are possible," (Matthew 19:26). Thus when we combine these two facts with the grace that God bestows upon us; perfection in the eyes of the Lord, and subsequently, "righteousness," is more than an achievable goal.

It was this belief that Job possessed that caused him to respond to Bildad with questions of his own. Four questions in fact:

"How have you helped him who is without power?" (26:2)

"How have you saved the arm that has no strength?" (26:2)

"How have you counseled one who has no wisdom?" (26:3)

"And how have you declared sound advice to many?" (26:3)

Simply put, Job is questioning how the words of Bildad could possibly provide someone with encouragement or support on their spiritual journey. It is like if a soccer coach comes out before the game and says, 'the team we are playing today is much higher than us on the table, there is no hope for us to beat them, they are better than us.' It becomes all the more unlikely in this case for the team to win the game if the coach himself lacks faith in their abilities. We have to learn to support each other on our spiritual paths and shepherd those friends of ours who may have lost their way a little bit. Job understands the weakness of humanity and if we are left to our own devices, we would

ghteousness

ighteousness is' one the chief attributes God as portrayed in Hebrew Bible. Its ef meaning concerns ical conduct (for mple, Leviticus 19:36; uteronomy 25:1; lm 1:6; Proverbs '0). In the Book of , the main character ntroduced to us as a person who is perfect In righteousness.

Hosts

The word 'hosts' is interchangeable with the word 'armies' in the Bible. Which is why we call God "the Lord of hosts" and Job claims that His armies are "innumerable."

People, Places &Things

What the Fathers Say

Man, helpless to conceive the secrets of God, stands in awe before the divine talk, as though before thunder, not able to apprehend its secret.

— St. Ambrose

fail in our quest for righteousness. But God, who is the Savior of all men, who pours down grace upon those who call upon it; holds the power to transform our hearts and renew our spirits towards seeking righteousness. "By His Spirit He adorned the heavens," (26:13). If this is true, can He not also restore our souls? If we believe this to be true then the analogy regarding the soccer coach carries a new meaning. If I am on a team that is struggling and a new coach is appointed, I need to believe that he holds the key to transforming our team so that we can enjoy success with him. Again, if I doubt his abilities to coach our team, then I am mocking his role as a coach. In the same way that if I doubt God's abilities to transform me, then I am mocking His role as a Redeemer.

This conversation eventually leads to the verse that defines the character of Job throughout all his sufferings as he says to Bildad, "My righteousness I hold fast, and will not let it go" (27:6). It was this

REFLECTION

Where do I go for strength and comfort in times of trials?

persistence in his righteousness that was so precious in the sight of God. We must learn from the perseverance of Job in the face of brutal allegations. No matter how much we are persecuted, we have to hold fast to our righteousness, this was his most valuable trait. That no matter how much he was accused and told that God had rejected him, he did not surrender his righteousness before God, but rather stood fast, even to the very end.

What the Fathers Say

Some of the fathers of the church believe that, as man alone among all creatures' looks upward and not downward, the Holy Spirit of God adorned the heaven, in order to draw man's sight upwards, so as not to be preoccupied with the earthly things. He set for him the seen heavens, with such a beauty, that, by faith, he may look up at the unseen heavens, in anticipation of his eternal dwelling place.

- Fr Tadros Malaty

CHAPTERS 28-31

Job's Final Discourse

Are you getting bored yet? I know I am. Pretty sure I delayed writing this part of the book for 2 years. Shout out to those who are still reading and if you are, then sit up straight, grab yourself a nice cup of coffee (or hot cocoa, I know that's my preference) and pay attention. Because here is where things get intense and beautiful. These are Job's final words in the book to his friends, so you best bet he is going to make the most of them.

Job began his final rebuttal in chapter 26 when responding to the condemning questions of Bildad and continues through to chapter 31. This final discourse can be broken up into 4 parts:

1. Chapter 28 – Praise of Wisdom

2. Chapter 29 – Mourning the loss of past wealth

3. Chapter 30 – Frustration towards his friends and God

4. Chapter 31 – A call for justice

With each passing word, we can almost hear the tearful complaint of Job getting louder and more desperate. It almost makes sense that God would show up after this complaint as He Himself proclaimed to the multitudes in Matthew 5:4, "Blessed are those who mourn for they shall be comforted." We can hear the pain in Job's final dialogue increasing as he first begins by singing the praises of wisdom and ends by begging for justice. There are so many treasures we can learn from his final words, so please read with a prayerful heart.

WHERE IS WISDOM FOUND?

After Job held fast to his righteousness, he encourages his friends to seek a voice of wisdom and understanding in this ordeal. He urges this so that their eyes may be opened to the honesty in his words as he truthfully exclaims, "what is hidden he brings forth to light," (28:11) pointing out the fact that the truth will be revealed one way or another. This holds true in our lives also, when at times we find ourselves in situations where our pleading for understanding hearts falls on deaf ears. How many times do we try and speak to people who are too stubborn to listen? But then again, how many times are we too stubborn to listen to certain people because they bear traits that are not in line with what we deem "wise"? Sometimes we feel as though some people cannot teach us anything and so we decide it's better to

mighty

e word "Almighty" is nslated as "Shaddai" Hebrew and was the aracteristic patriarchal ne used for God by Job oughout his struggle.

Trivia

Throughout the entire book of Job, there is not a single mention of the following significant Jewish things: Israel, the exodus from Egypt, the Mosaic Law, the Tabernacle.

People, Places &Things

just close our ears to them. This is identical to the Pharisees who covered their ears to the words of the Lord, believing He didn't have the capacity to teach them due to the hardness of their hearts. Where the world says, "you cannot be taught," Wisdom says: "you can learn from anyone and anything." It is important for us to always have an understanding mind in all situations in order to learn. Pope Shenouda III exemplifies this wisdom in his book called "Discipleship" where he speaks about a sparrow and learning from the habits of this sparrow. He says, "Believe me, I've learned many lessons from the sparrows! I was sitting before my cell in the monastery garden once, and there were a few seeds on the ground, which might have been dropped by one of the farm workers. A sparrow came to feed on the seeds, and I imagined that it would eat until it had had its fill from this source of provision. But it took one or two seeds and flew off, leaving all this goodness behind without minding or regretting it. And so I learned a lesson from this about frugality and being satisfied with what one has, and in fact about detachment as well." So we learn a valuable lesson, that if a Pope can learn from a bird, then wisdom can teach us anything through the lives of anyone, even our enemies. Where is wisdom found? With God, for "God understands its way, and He knows its place." (28:23). If we find God, who is Wisdom as Solomon says in Proverbs, then we will live with understanding hearts towards everyone all our days.

POSITION OF BROKENNESS

Job continues his complaint by mourning the loss of his past wealth saying, "Oh that I were as in months past, when His lamp shone over my head," (29:2). It is here where Job misunderstands the nature of God, claiming that because he was no longer prospering, God had abandoned him, continuing, "Just as I was in the days of my prime, when the friendly counsel of God was over my tent," (29:4). This is a trap we should never fall into, believing that God has forsaken us in times of hardship. He was the one who promised us, "in the world you will have tribulation; but be of good cheer, I have overcome the WORLD," (John 16:33). Not only has Christ promised to overcome our tribulations, but the whole world, every aspect of our lives, He will overcome. So immediately, we notice the first error in the ways of Job's complaint, believing that God had left him in his time of tribulation.

His next error is perhaps more flawed however, as he exclaims, "When the ear heard, then it blessed me, and when the eye saw, then it approved me; because I delivered the poor who cried out, the fatherless and the one who had no helper," (29:11-12). What is Job implying here? Is he implying that his wealth was a result of his good deeds? Yes, but there is more. He is also suggesting that because he was living in a state of prosperity, he was able to serve those who were not. Now that he is not, he can't do so anymore. But is this true? Is this what we are taught as

> ## What the Fathers Say
>
> *God did not just make us wise, righteous, and saints in Christ; He, above all that, gave us Christ for the sake of our salvation.*
>
> *– St. John Chrysostom*

Christians? To only serve when are living in richness? Of course not! Fr. Yacoub Magdy once said that, "God puts us in positions of brokenness so we can help others who are also suffering." The greatest example of this was Christ Himself who served most when He was being scourged and crucified. In the midst of being betrayed, He healed Malchus. In the midst of carrying His cross, He comforted the weeping women. In the midst of hanging, bleeding and bruised on a cross, He looked down and left His mother in the care of His beloved disciple John. So in the time that Christ was most broken and had every right to worry about Himself, He was constantly looking around to see whom else He could help, who else He could serve. We are called to do likewise. D.T Niles states, "Evangelism is witness. It is one beggar telling another beggar where to get food." We are all empty of something, broken in one way or another, just like beggars, but that should never stop us from serving others around us. No matter how broken we may be, no matter how much we are suffering, we should always look at our state as an opportunity to serve someone who is in more need.

When you suffer anything even half as bad as Job suffered, there will be moments of frustration and anger that arise no doubt. After an extended period of time arguing with his 'friends,' this moment finally comes for Job in the form of exceptional arrogance when he states, "But now they mock at me, men younger than I, whose fathers I disdained to put with the dogs of my flock," (30:1). The way Job was treated by his friends was miserable, to say the least, but no amount of mockery could ever justify such an arrogant statement from Job's behalf that he wouldn't even allow their fathers to be in the presence of his dogs. Surely we are taught to respond differently? Again if we look at Christ's example on the cross in the height of his pain, what did he say about those who persecuted Him? "Father, forgive them, for they do not know what they do," (Luke 23:34). He showed forgiveness! In the face of those who scourged Him, mocked Him, beat Him, bruised Him and humiliated Him... He forgave them! We underestimate the power of forgiveness in our daily lives. On March 12th 2015, 21 Libyan men were abducted while they were away at work and martyred in a publicised act of violence. Some days later, a news reporter visited the families of those men who were killed and asked them about their thoughts on the murderers who killed their brothers, sons, husbands, fathers etc. The response was a language of forgiveness. "I thank the man who killed my husband," one woman said, "I can now say that I am the wife of a martyr." This is the language with which we ought to speak. Why? Because it moves the hearts of people. Why did the right hand thief convert? Was it because he saw the sky thunder and the ground quake as we sometimes suggest? No! That all happened afterwards. He converted because he heard the loving words of our Saviour on the cross, forgiving those who placed Him there.

WAITING ON THE LORD

Job, however, rather than speaking gently about his friends, continues by saying, "they were sons of fools, yes, sons of vile men," (30:8). His frustration was not restricted to his friends alone, escalating to the point where he began accusing God even. "I cry out to You, but You do not answer me; I stand up and You regard me. But You have become cruel to me; with the strength of Your hand You oppose me," (30:20-21). These accusations of God seemingly abandoning him continue for the remainder of chapter 30; Job complaining that this is the cause of his mourning. They are very harsh words to say against our Lord, that He has become "cruel" to Job. Is it even in the capacity of such a gracious God for Him to be cruel? Do the sufferings that Job endured give him the right to be so harsh with God? Sometimes I feel as though the sufferings that Job experienced, whilst excruciating, still do not compare with the sufferings of Joseph the son of Jacob. Joseph, was only a teenage boy when he had his whole world taken away from him as he was sold to the Egyptians. Just when he had started to get his life back on track, he was then thrown into prison under false accusations and remained there for 17 years. Instead of blaming God, or sulking, or whinging, Joseph used this time to grow in stature before God and man, using his time in prison for the glory of God by interpreting dreams and serving all those in the prisons with him. Not once did Joseph accuse God of being too cruel against him, but rather, he remained steadfast in his faith and above all else, he was patient. Waiting for the deliverance of the Lord that he knew would surely come. Just as King David sang in Psalm 130, "I wait for the Lord, my soul waits for the Lord, more than those who watch for the morning," we are called to be patient in our trials. There is a promise that comes to those who are patient in another one of David's psalms which says, "Wait on the Lord; be of good courage, and He shall strengthen your heart; wait, I say, on the Lord!" (Psalm 27:14). So whenever we are suffering, just "wait", God has something amazing in store for us just around the corner.

SELF-EXAMINATION

Job ends his words with a thorough self-examination of all the sins that his friends accused him of and in light of that, calls for justice. What is curious about this chapter is the way Job speaks of his virtues openly to try and disrepute the allegations made against him. It may seem obnoxious, or even somewhat arrogant, but it isn't. In fact, we are called to self-evaluate our lives always so we may observe where our flaws lie and where we can improve to continue our spiritual growth. Observing that we have gained certain virtues along the way of our spiritual journey is not a testimony to our greatness or perceived holiness, but rather a tribute to the grace of God. In St Paul's first letter to the Corinthians

> ## What the Fathers Say
>
> *Having talked about his past days of prosperity, and the terror dwelling now on him; 'Job' starts now searching his depths, lest he may probably have committed hidden sins as claimed by his friends! The self-search 'Job' conducted was not in the light of the law which was not delivered yet to the prophet Moses; But in the light of the Holy Bible. According to which, he proclaims that he is ready to answer any question that God may ask him.*
>
> *— Fr. Tadros Malaty*

he echoes this notion by saying, "By the grace of God I am what I am," (1 Cor. 15:10). John the Baptist himself acknowledged who he was and his purpose here on earth when he responded to those questioning whether or not he was the Messiah by claiming, "I am 'the voice of one crying in the wilderness: make straight the way of the Lord' as the prophet Isaiah said," (John 1:23). Arrogant? No, but a witness to the grace of God working in their lives for the glory of His name.

Some of the virtues that Job openly confesses to owning include:

- The purity of his eyes – "I have made a covenant with my eyes." (31:1).

- His preoccupation with God – "For what is the allotment of God from above, and the portion from the Almighty on high?   (31: 2).

- His uprightness – "If I have walked with falsehood, or if my foot has hastened to deceit, Let me be weighed on honest scales, that God may know my integrity" (31:5).

- His care for the lowly of society – "If I have kept the poor from their desire, or cause the eyes of the widow to fall... Then let my arm fall from my shoulder" (31:16; 22).

- His rejection of riches for the sake of God – "If I made gold my hope...

this would be an iniquity deserving of judgment, for I would have denied God who is above." (31:24; 28).

These and many others are included in Job's final speech riddled with the many qualities of Job. And because of all these attributes he claims to have, Job makes a final, pleading cry for justice saying, "Let me be weighed in honest scales, that God may know my integrity," (31:6). It's a slight echo of his cry at the beginning of his dialogue with his friends when he said, "Oh, that my grief were fully weighed, and my calamity laid with it on the scales!" (Job 6:2). What is this obsession Job has with scales? This is actually a direct call for the Lord to deliver on his promise of a righteous judgment for all His people. God first made this promise in the time of Moses when He proclaimed, "You shall have honest scales, honest weights, an honest ephah, and an honest hin," (Leviticus 19:36). God repeats this promise yet again to the princes of Israel in the book of Ezekiel when He says, "You shall have honest scales, an honest ephah, and an honest bath," (Ezekiel 45:10). Just like Job, we are all standing on these scales of His. Sometimes we feel heavier when it feels as though we are carrying the weight of the world on our shoulders, other times we feel light, as though that weight has been lifted. It is God's scale and so it's His choice to decide what we can bear while we stand on those scales, as it says in the book of Proverbs, "Honest weights and scales are the Lord's;

All the weights in the bag are His work," (Proverbs 16:11). Christ decides to bestow upon us heavier burdens to carry so that His handiwork could be revealed through us. This is similar to the story of the blind man in the gospel of John. When the disciples asked Christ, "who sinned, this man or his parents, that he was born blind? Jesus answered, "Neither this man nor his parents sinned, but that the works of God should be revealed in him," (John 9:2-3). It is the decision of God when it feels like the weight on our scales is unbearably hefty, but it is through that substantial weight that the works of God are revealed in our lives, just like in the life of the blind man and just as we will shortly see in the life of Job.

REFLECTION

What am I most attached to in this world? If God asked me to give it up, could I do it easily or would I struggle?

CHAPTER 32

CHAPTER 32

Events

ELIHU THE YOUNGEST SPEAKS

It is at this point of the story where the three 'friends' of Job finally give up. Their arguing with Job comes to an end at long last. The reason for this is actually quite astonishing. In the biblical text we have it read as, "So these three men ceased answering Job, because he was righteous in his own eyes," (32:1). This text, in the Septuagint, the Syrian, the old Arabic, and the Chaldean versions, reads as: "because he was righteous in (their) eyes". And in the version by Symmachus, it reads as: "because he proved to be more righteous than them." In any case, they came to the sound conclusion that Job was indeed a righteous man and their accusations were baseless. Then Elihu shows up.

The name 'Elihu' means 'God is Jehovah'. His name, just like his character, both declares his role as a messenger from God to Job, to prepare him to enjoy seeing God, who will come in the whirlwind. Elihu bears a shadow of Christ who is to come and intercede for us all. This is important to know because Elihu's role in this story of Job is to deliver the message of God. This and other factors make Elihu different from the other friends of Job:

1.   He is the youngest of them all – "I am young in years, and you are very old," (32:6) he told them.

2. He does not condemn Job for thinking of himself to be righteous, but for

thinking of himself to be righteous with his own justification rather than leaning on the defense of the Lord – "his wrath was aroused because he justified himself rather than God," (32:2).

3. His message was not his own, but God's – "there is a spirit in man, and the breath of the Almighty gives him understanding." (32:8).

SPEAKING THE TRUTH

If we are to learn one thing from Elihu it's this: when the Spirit of God induces within you the desire to speak the truth, don't let any obstacles get in your way or give you excuses to be silent. Elihu himself confesses that he knows his young age is a hindrance to him and that because of his youth Job and the three men may choose to ignore him – but he doesn't let that stop him. In fact he says of this, "the Spirit within me compels me," (32:18). I was once sitting on a beach with my brother-in-law and he turned around and said to me, "all these people sitting on this beach

ymmachus

ymmachus translated he Old Testament into Greek in the late 2nd entury. His translation was included by Origen in his Hexapla nd Tetrapla, which ompared various ersions of the Old Testament side by side with the Septuagint. He was also heavily admired by Jerome, who used his work in composing the 'Vulgate.'

People, Places &Things

What the Fathers Say

This wisdom and reason are found in Christ; and by Him we get to know God the Father and see Him. All the wisdom of this world, out of, or without Christ, is counted as lowly, void, and of no real value.

– Father Maruis Victorinus

need to meet Christ." I decided I'd ignore the apparent ignorance of the statement and asked him "why?" He responded, "It's our job!" People long to hear the truth of Christ, people who are broken, sad, alone, concerned, stressed and living in all sorts of darkness, surround us. These are the people who need the light of Christ in their lives, and it is our duty that they experience it. Fr. Tadros Yacoub Malaty says that we must pray "to be jealous for the salvation of all those around us." How many times do we stop ourselves from speaking about Christ because we are embarrassed? Or how many times do I choose not to mention that I am a Christian so that I won't be excluded from popular social circles? We need conviction in our faith to speak up boldly. You don't think you can make a difference, change the world even? Maybe not, but Mother Teresa says, "I may not be able to change the world, but I can cast a stone in the waters to create many ripples." Maybe you're concerned you won't know what to tell people. However, in Mark 13:11 Christ promises, "It is not you who speak, but the Holy Spirit." Elihu didn't have this promise, and he didn't even have the Holy Spirit inside of him, but God gave him conviction to speak Truth and he didn't silence it – neither should we.

EDIFYING TALK

Another virtue that is admirable in Elihu's character is his patience as he claims, "I waited for your words," speaking to Job and his friends, "I listened to your reasoning while you searched out what to say" (32:11). Elihu teaches us a lesson taught in Ecclesiastes, that there is a time to speak and a time to keep silent. Oftentimes we will find ourselves in needless arguments because we are too rash to speak our minds. If we however give others the chance to share their points of view, we will find that they will give us the same respect and hence, avoid getting into a heated dispute. This is also a form of peacemaking that we humble ourselves in silence even if we feel that someone else was in the wrong. The most condemning part of his statement was his claim that Job's friends "searched out what to say." It is almost as though he is telling them, 'your words were aimless, you don't care to help Job, you only care to find the right words to condemn him.' They did not seek to edify, only to debate. St Anthony warns us, "If you encounter someone who loves to debate issues that are obvious facts and known truth; you should cut the talk on the spot, and quit; because his mind has turned into stone! Just as water can destroy a solid rock, foolish debate can corrupt the behavior and nature of good men." The lesson is, never argue for the sake of arguing. Always seek to edify. A beautiful thing I learnt from the life of Samuel the prophet was that he never uttered a word that was 'useless,' so to speak. It says of him that, "the Lord was with him and let none of his words fall to the ground," (1 Sam. 3:19) suggesting that every word he spoke was inspired from the

> ## What the Fathers Say
>
> Whoever foolishly speaks is brainless, as he speaks without prior thinking over all issues. Therefore, examine all what is for your benefit, to do it for your own salvation.
>
> – St. Anthony the Great

Lord. This is similar to Elihu's approach here. He says, "Now he has not directed his words against me; So I will not answer him with your words" (32:14). What Elihu is saying is that since Job has not spoken a word against him, his conviction to speak is not due to any partiality or resentment but rather, out of pure desire to speak the truth as he follows up by saying, "The spirit within me compels me," (32:18). May we ask the Lord to grant us the same edifying speech, so that our tongue may never be a source of destruction to the nature of good men but rather an instrument for Truth.

REFLECTION

Can you think of a time when you spoke too soon and it caused you probems?

CHAPTER 33

The Sweetness of Salvation

Perhaps, out of every word Elihu spoke, the words in this particular chapter were of the highest magnificence. Maybe even the most remarkable in the entire book of Job in regards to the reference made to God as the eternal Mediator. Such were the importance of his words that he pleads with Job both at the beginning and end of this chapter to heed his words. He begins by saying, "Please, Job, hear my speech, and listen to all my words," (33:1) and ends with, "Give ear, Job, listen to me," (33:31). Almost as if to say, 'if you understand nothing else, at least understand these words I say right now, for they are most pertinent to your salvation.' I guess this in itself is a lesson we can learn for ourselves in the early stages of our spiritual lives. When reading the Bible or listening to a sermon, make an effort to take at least one important lesson from what is being said and apply that lesson in your life. Sometimes if we take on too much at once we can lose motivation or worse, not apply it heartily. Think back to the earlier story we mentioned about Pope Shenouda and the sparrow. The bird only took a small portion of the abundant seeds that he had left for it to indulge in. Not only that, but the bird left without taking any seeds to have for later, despite not knowing where its next meal would come from. We should take just enough to be fulfilled and trust that it will be sufficient for us and that God will provide what we need when we need

CHAPTER 33

it. So, with every sermon and with every book you read (including this one if possible), try and find the seeds that will be sufficient for you in your life of prayer.

Elihu goes on to make a statement that many of the church fathers use as evidence which confirms the divinity of the Holy Spirit playing a part as a Creator of life saying, "The Spirit of God has made me, and the breath of the Almighty gives me life" (Job 33:4). Here Elihu eliminates any sense of distinction between him and Job informing him that, as a creation of the Spirit of God, he is just a tool in His hands of God, the same God who created and breathed life into Job also. He follows this up by saying, "I also have been formed out of clay" (Job 22: 6), as a reminder to Job that they are both indebted to the Spirit of God for their existence and life; both are His creation, and both have the same nature, and the same weaknesses, therefore Job should not fear hearing the words of his fellow man.

Throughout the course of the entire book, Job made some harsh accusations against God as Elihu reminded him. Calling him his "enemy" and saying that He put his "feet in the stocks," to name only a couple. Elihu responds to this harshness by telling Job, "in this you are not righteous", why? "For God is greater than man," (33:12). Who am I that I should argue against the Creator of the whole world? Imagine a MacBook telling Steve Jobs how to use it – it's ridiculous! Steve Jobs knows the ins and outs of the MacBook because he created it, he can use it however he pleases. It is a concept mentioned in the book of Isaiah from the mouth of God who speaks and says, "For My thoughts are not your thoughts, nor are your ways My ways," (Is 55:8). Who am I to question God? As Elihu says, "God may speak in one way or another, yet man does not perceive it," (33:14). We may not understand why God is doing something in our lives at a given time, but we need to trust that it is for our salvation. He allows us to suffer "in order to turn man from his deed and conceal man from his pride," (33:17). This is God's role as the Mediator in our lives. He intervenes in order to save us from this "Pit" that Elihu speaks of. It's like a parent who places restrictions on their children such as, 'don't play on the streets!' We may not understand the rule, we may get angry at the limitations placed upon us, but as we grow older we see that it was for our own benefit. God may intervene in one way or another, 'yet we may not perceive it,' with time however, all will be made clear.

People, Places &Things

Cultural influence

The Book of Job has been deeply influential in Western culture. Many artworks, musical pieces, literature and even films have drawn on the themes and storyline from the book for inspiration and dedication. Musical settings from Job include Orlande de Lassus's 1565 cycle motets, the Sacrae Lec. Novem ex Propheta Jo. George Frideric Hand. use of Job 19:25 ("I kr that my redeemer livet. an aria in his 1741 orc Messiah.

HOW GOD INTERVENES

The ways in which God intervenes are unique also. Each person's experiences and interactions with God will be different to the person next to them. This is the really beautiful thing I find in our relationship with God – that it is truly personal. It is MY relationship with God. And here Elihu consolidates that by mentioning 5 different ways in which God intervenes in our lives:

1. The first is through dreams & visions, "when deep sleep falls upon men," (33:15). It was in this way that God intervened in the life of Joseph, by giving him the gift of interpreting dreams in order that he may be saved. The key part – 'in order that he may be saved.' It is important to remember that.

2. The second is through hidden inspiration as Elihu says that at any given time, "He opens the ears of man," (33:16). We have all been granted this particular gift in regards to the Gospel. In the Litany of the Gospel during the liturgy the priest will tell the congregation, "Blessed are your eyes for they see and your ears for they hear." We must use this occasion as a chance for renewal, to not just hear the word, but to understand and apply.

3. The third is through grief. "Man is also chastened with pain on his bed," (33:19). Possibly this one pertains mainly to Job and his suffering. We know that God granted Job

> **What the Fathers Say**
>
> Speaking about the Redeemer Christ, Elihu lifts our sight up from the afflictions, the grievances, and the infirmity, to what we enjoy through that amazing redemption.
>
> – Fr. Tadros Malaty

grief so that he may prove his righteousness in the face of adversity and hence prove his love for Him. It's vital that we remember this whenever we face similar trials – that we take that period of grief as an opportunity to prove our love for God.

What the Fathers Say

The Mediator between God and man, the Lord Jesus Christ, who took the form of Man; in His compassion, says to His Father on the account of man to be saved: "Spare him from going down to the pit of corruption".

– St. Gregory the Great

4. The fourth is by Heavenly mediation with Elihu mentioning that there may be "a messenger for him" (33:23) whom God wishes to save. Before the battle against Jericho, Joshua "lifted up his eyes and looked, and behold a Man stood opposite him with His sword drawn in His hand. And Joshua went to Him and said to Him, 'Are You for us or for our adversaries?' So He said, 'No, but as a Commander of the army of the Lord I have now come,'" (Joshua 5:13-14). A messenger was sent to Joshua with a strategy that would gain victory and salvation for the Israelites.

5. And finally, but by no means the least, Elihu says, "Deliver him from going down to the Pit; for I have found a ransom," (33:24). What was this ransom? The blood of Christ. Christ confirmed to His disciples that His life was to be the ultimate mediation when He told them, "For even the Son of Man did not come to be served, but to serve, and to give His life a ransom for many," (Mark 10:45). And thus, the blood of Christ has become the decisive intervention in our lives to save us from the Pit, for without it, the others are futile, but because of it, we have been saved.

The most wonderful thing about Christ intervening in our life is tasting the sweetness of His salvation for us. For the one who experiences the salvation of God, "His life shall be young like a child's, he shall return to the days of his youth. He shall pray to God, and He will delight in him, he shall see His face with joy, for He restores to man His righteousness," (33:25-26). Can you imagine how joyful these words would have been for Job to hear? And for each of us also! Sure, maybe my struggles today place a burden on my shoulders I can no longer stand to bear. Maybe it feels like I'm deep in a Pit of my own anxiety, or concerns, or fears. But we must always remember, "that the sufferings of this present time are not worthy to be compared with the glory which shall be revealed in us," (Rom 8:18). Or put in a more fitting way, 'the pit I am in today is not worthy to be compared with the sweetness of God's salvation for me.'

REFLECTION

Do I use times of sadness in my life as an opportunity to draw closer to God, or am I so consumed by my grief that I ignore Him?

CHAPTERS 34-36

"TEACH ME WHAT I DO NOT SEE!"

The first speech of Elihu, which we've just explored, was directed towards Job. We notice at the beginning of chapter 34 that Elihu turns towards the friends of Job and directs his speech to them, without receiving a response from Job. There are two possible reasons that scholars believe to be the reason Job did not respond to him. The first is that he disregarded his speech altogether out of disrespect for Elihu was younger than him. Although the second, and more likely reason, is that he was fearful of having to endure more condemning questions from all those who were present. Whatever the reason, it meant that Elihu could now turn his attention to the rest of the audience (Job's friends) and begin his second talk. Between chapters 34 and 36, Elihu delivers three more talks.

1. In 34 he speaks to the friends regarding the ordinances of God and teaches all those present how to talk to God.

2. In 35 he speaks to all of them explaining the prayers that go un-received.

3. In 36 Elihu glorifies God's righteousness and prepares the way for His appearance.

APPROACHING OTHERS WISELY

Elihu begins his speech in a very shrewd way, a way that for sure captured the attentiveness of Job's friends by referring to

Events

CHAPTERS 34-36

them as "wise men... who have knowledge," (34:2). In a book by Dale Carnegie called, "How to win friends and influence people," he speaks about gaining people's respect by sincerely making them feel important. "The deepest principle in human nature is the craving to feel appreciated. Most people you meet feel themselves to be superior to you in some way, let them realize in some subtle way that you recognize their importance, and recognize it sincerely," he writes. This is the easiest way to grasp someone's attention – not by dishonest or superficial flattery, but by recognizing his or her strengths and virtues.

Elihu then comments on Job saying, "I am righteous, but God has taken away my justice," (34:5) which he previously claimed in chapter 13:18 and 27:2. While a lot of Job's words were harsh accusations against God throughout the course of his sufferings, the fathers don't believe these words were said as an allegation against God's justice or even to justify himself, but rather that God allowed

---

wish usage of Job

wish liturgy does not use adings from the Book of b in the manner of the ntateuch, Prophets, or ve Megillot, although 's quoted at funerals d times of mourning. wever, there are some vs, particularly the anish and Portuguese

Jews, who do hold public readings of Job on the Tisha B'Av fast (a day of mourning over the destruction of the First and Second Temples and other tragedies).

People, Places &Things

his friends to see guilt and not innocence in his character. As the book progresses in this ever constant theme of "you are guilty – no I am not!" dialogue, we learn an extremely valuable lesson on silence. That lesson is: so long as God stays silent through my trials, so must I! Going back to that teacher in an exam analogy, how the teacher stays silent during the test does not also the student? What will it profit me if I try to prove my own innocence in a court of law when my witness is still silent? God is the only witness to my righteousness and I must trust that in His acceptable time, He will testify on my behalf. For me, I must consider that there is, "a time to keep silence and a time to speak," (Ecc 3:7). It's important to remember also that Christ Himself kept silent through His trials.

WE ARE OF EQUAL VALUE

What Elihu goes on to emphasise to them is that God is not a God who can even be associated with wrongdoing, "Far be it from God to do wickedness," (34:10) he says. If we are punished it is not out of the wickedness of God, which does not exist, but because of our own iniquities as he also says, "He repays man according to his work," (34:11). We forget too often that God is the One who gave us life and that, "If He should gather to Himself His Spirit and His breath," which He gave to us freely, "all flesh would perish together," (34:14). We forget this because that is not the character of God that we are accustomed to. The God we know is gentle and loving in nature, One who cares for each of our trivial intricacies. He's numbered every hair on our heads! Why? Because to God we are not just insignificant creatures that He would dispose of at the first hint of disobedience, to God we are pearls of great price, worthy of selling an entire field to purchase (Matthew 13:45-46). "Nor does He regard the rich more than the poor, for they are all the work of His hands," (34:19) meaning we are all of equal value in the eyes of God no matter our material wealth or success.

There was once a teacher who stood up in front of the class holding a $20 note and asked a student if they wanted the note. The student replied "of course!" The teacher then crumpled up the note and asked the student again if they wanted the note to which he got the same answer. Finally, the teacher stepped on the note and asked again, and again received the same answer. Why? Because even though the note was now crumpled up, stepped on and become dirty, it still held its value as $20. It's the same thing with us in our relationship with God. No matter how bruised we may be, how broken, how scarred, we will always hold the same priceless value to our Lord who will desire to have us no matter how we approach Him.

TEACH ME WHAT I DO NOT SEE

There are then seven words at the end of chapter 34 that Elihu tells us to say to God whenever we approach Him in prayer, "Teach me what I do not see," (34:31). 'Show me Lord

What the Fathers Say

In your life, as it is in that of every believer, there are sins hidden from your eyes, that you involuntarily practice, and yet cannot see or realise. Seek from God to reveal them to you.

— Fr. Tadros Malaty

my shortcomings, my flaws, my iniquities, my sins!!' It is a prayer that has been encouraged by Fr. Matthew the Poor who also says, "When you pray, ask the Lord, 'expose my sins O Lord, so that I can remove whatever it is that separates me from You.'" If we are serious about our spiritual lives then this is a prayer we must constantly fall back on, in order to be continuously striving for a deeper relationship with God. When Moses saw God in the burning bush, the Lord requested from Moses to, "take his sandals off his feet," (Exodus 3:5). The reason as we all know is because the place he stood was holy ground, but I don't think that's all. Perhaps another reason the Lord wanted Moses to take his sandals off his feet was that so there was no separation between them. We all wear sandals in our lives that do us no harm but without them, we may find ourselves drawing much nearer to God. Some people wear sandals of their friends, others sandals of their career. Today and everyday, we must learn to ask God to reveal to us what these sandals in our lives are by asking "teach me what I do not see," so that we can remove them and be closer to Him as a consequence.

"If you are righteous, what do you give Him? Or what does He receive from your hands?" (35:7). It's a fair question, what do we offer God if we do well? There is nothing that God needs from us, He is already infinite, we cannot add to that. Elihu asks this damning question basically to tell Job, 'stop using your righteousness as an accusation against God's justice.' Our righteousness is not a favor to God, in fact, if we are righteous in any way; it is because of the grace of God. As King David writes, "My goodness is nothing apart from You," (Psalm 16:2). The reason we attain righteousness is for our own good, that we may gain the heavenly reward, not earthly relief. "If you are wise, you are wise for yourself," (Proverbs 9:12). Think about your parents: yes they want you to study, yes they are pleased when you do well in your exams, but what do your good results add to their lives? Do they need you to do well in your exams? (Some might argue yes) but the truth is they really don't – it is for your own good! Likewise with our righteousness – it is our obligation to be righteous as Christians, but God forbid we should ever think our righteousness is for God's benefit, rather we should say like the servants in the parable of the plowers, "we are unprofitable servants. We have done what was our duty to do," (Luke 17:10).

THE UNANSWERED PRAYER

Growing up in the church we are taught that God hears and answers all our prayers, but there is a prayer that God refuses to answer, even in our deepest need. That is the prayer of a proud heart as Elihu comments, "There they cry out, but He does not answer, because of the pride of evildoers" (35:12). It's just as in the story of the Pharisee and the Tax Collector. The reason one prayer was answered and not the other because one was said in a spirit of humility and contrition and the other in a spirit of pride. We know that "God resists the proud but gives grace to the humble" (James 4:6) and whenever I read this verse I imagine someone who has just eaten garlic. The common thing that occurs to anyone who's just indulged in a garlic-tainted meal is that they smell really bad. No one wants to be near them. Pride is just like garlic to the Lord. Sure, He still loves you, but He doesn't want to be anywhere near you. If your words are not filled with humility then your words become empty to Him and, "God will not listen to empty talk," (35:13).

Finally, Elihu begins to prepare the way for God's entrance into this story by "ascribing righteousness to his Maker," (36:3) and clarifying to Job that the Almighty One will never stop dealing justly with mankind, comforting him by saying, "He does not withdraw His eyes from the righteous," (36:7). This infinite justice of God is really quite reassuring to us. I will probably sound like a broken record by saying this but the saying is true, that even if the whole world thinks of me as an unrighteous man, God will testify for my righteousness in His appropriate time. This is exactly what Elihu is trying to tell Job – 'God sees your righteousness Job; His eyes are not turned away from you just because your friends don't see it. Have faith and all will be revealed in the right time.' All that is necessary for us in our lives, is to live a righteous life before God – like Zacchariah and Elizabeth who we read about earlier.

WHO WILL YOU BRING WITH YOU?

What I love about Elihu is that he knew he was not the full stop in the sufferings of Job, he was merely a colon, preparing the way for God to come in and restore Job. He says, "there are yet words to speak on God's behalf," (36:2) before defending His righteousness to prepare for Him to enter. This is in fact our calling as Christians. We are called to prepare the way for the Lord. St John the Beloved says of St John the Baptist that "this man came for a witness, to bear witness of the Light, that all through him might believe," (John 1:7). St John the Baptist was not the Light, but he pointed towards the Light so that all his followers would find Christ. He prepared the way. Christ Himself when He instructed His disciples to go and preach, it says that He, "sent them out two by two before His face into every place where He Himself was about to go," (Luke 10:1). The disciples went first and Christ followed. They prepared the way. We are called to plant and water; it is Christ who gives the increase (1 Cor. 3:6). There is a really lovely picture that was once painted by a servant in a sermon, where he spoke about the day we all go to Heaven. He said that on that day, God would ask each of us whom we brought with us. On that day, he said, St Anthony will point to all the monks whom he prepared the way for. On that day, St Mark will point to all the Coptic Christians

What the Fathers Say

The sick need a Savior. The lost need a Guide. The blind need someone to lead them to light. The thirsty need a living Fountain; He who drinks from it, would never thirst. The dead need life. The sheep need a Shepherd. The children need a Teacher. And all humanity needs Jesus.

– St. Clement of Alexandria

whom he prepared the way for. The question that comes to us today is: whom will I point to on that day? For whom have I prepared the way to Christ? Elihu offers a word of advice as to how we can prepare this way as he begins drawing to a close his honorable speech saying, "Remember to magnify His work, of which men have sung. Everyone has seen it; man looks on it from afar," (36:24-26). Magnify the works of the Lord in your own life – live a life of love, peace and joy, so that all who see you may find and glorify God through you – then on the last day, you can turn and point towards them.

REFLECTION

What are the obstacles in my life that prevent me from having a deep relationship with God?

CHAPTER 37

THE APPROACHING STORM

The final verse of chapter 36 hints at a "rising storm" suggesting that God's whirlwind, from which He will speak to Job, has begun. Elihu, seeing this happening, elevates his mind and his heart from speaking about the earthly circumstances surrounding him and begins talking about this divine presence in a state of wonder. He says in admiration, "At this also my heart trembles, and leaps from its place" (37: 1). His heart leaps from contemplating on the sufferings of Job and begins meditating on the near presence of God; he forsakes the lowly things and concentrates on the things above. This begins a beautiful, poetic monologue by Elihu about God's authority over nature.

There are countless occasions in the Bible where God's voice is associated with a storm of some sorts. In the David's song of deliverance he says, "The Lord thundered from heaven, And the Most High uttered His voice" (2 Sam 22:14). It was said by the prophet Jeremiah, "When He utters His voice there is a tumult of waters in the heavens, and He makes the mist rise from the ends of the earth, He makes lightning for the rain, and He brings out the wind from His storehouses" (Jeremiah 10: 13, 16). King David also says that "the God of Glory thunders" (Ps 29:3), and that "the voice of the Lord shakes the wilderness" (Ps 29:8), revealing to us how His voice is a cause of trembling for His people. That trembling turns to sweetness when we

CHAPTER 37

learn to lift our hearts to the heavenly things and not be so consumed by the lowly things of the world. It is almost as though His voice thunders purposely in order that we may wake up to ourselves. God is not only in the natural whirlwind but He also stirs up an inner whirlwind of our souls, prompting us to seek peace from the innermost storms of our hearts through His Word. St Augustine says of this idea, "our hearts are restless Lord until they find rest in You."

There is a story of a group of youth who went on a missionary trip to Kenya and went around the villages visiting homes and preaching the word of God. They entered one home and found a man who was extremely unwelcoming and hostile, asking them multiple times to leave. After finally convincing him, he allowed them to stay and to read a passage from one of the Gospels. They read to him the story of Jesus calming the sea from the storms which plagued the boat in which Him and His disciples were sailing. After completing the story one of the youth shared a contemplation saying, "sometimes each of us has a storm of some sorts raging in our hearts, we need to wake up the Lord within us, just as the disciples did, for He alone can calm that tempest within us." The man, who was now in a flood of tears responded saying, "Today, I was planning to commit suicide, but God brought you all to my home in order that you may bring peace to the storm raging inside me." The Lord visits us in a thunderous

What the Fathers Say

Once you are in such a condition, you become captivated from your mind, to have Him alone, appear before your mind, in case it is capable of doing it; and if it is not, He would perpetually stay in memory. That way, man's mind would always become preoccupied with thinking about God and meditating in Him; a state called by our fathers 'keeping the mind'; surpassed by nothing among the virtues and all works.

- St. John of Dalyatha

storm so that we may learn to seek His face and beg for tranquility.

Elihu continues his speech proclaiming that God "does great things which we cannot comprehend" (37:5), pointing out His power over the heavy rains (37:6), His conduction of the winds (37:9), His creation of the ice and waters (37:10) and His jurisdiction over the clouds (37:11-12). He follows this by saying "He causes it to come, whether for correction, or for His land, or for mercy" (37:13) to imply that God never does anything haphazardly. This should have been extremely comforting for Job in his predicament. If God is all-powerful over creation and causes the winds to turn with motive, then why would He allow Job to suffer without reason? Elihu is reminding Job that his suffering has a purpose, and in his youthful wisdom he doesn't suggest any purpose (like the older friends tried to do). He simply stated that God will reveal that purpose to him in one way or another just as He will surely do with us in our time of trial.

"Listen to this, O Job; Stand still and

People, Places &Things

Clouds

The Hebrew definition of 'cloud,' so rendered means, "a covering," because clouds cover the sky. The word is used as a symbol of the Divine presence, as indicating the splendour of that glory which it conceals.

The Lord travelled before Israel after the Exodus from Egypt in the form of a "cloudy pillar," and the first mention of a cloud in the book of Job is found in chapter 22:14.

consider the wondrous works of God" (37:14).

In Elihu's final words to Job, he offers him a wise piece of advice – "stand still!" He tells him to be less concerned about his sufferings and to spend time in the presence of God, reflecting on His wonderful works. He asks him, "Do you know the balance of clouds, those wondrous works of Him who is perfect in knowledge?" (37:16), reminding him that God works in mysterious ways; and instead of questioning God's dealings with him, just trust that your life is being "weighed on honest scales" before God who is infinitely fair and just. Job, who had been debating with God up until this point is then asked by Elihu, "Teach us what we should say to Him, for we can prepare nothing because of the darkness" (37:19). This is very humble of Elihu as he is basically saying, "who am I to even whisper in the sight of God? But if you can speak up to the God of infinite wisdom, then teach me to be wise like you also that I may approach Him to talk to Him also."

REFLECTION

Is it difficult for me to see God's hand in my life, or do I see Him working in everything around me?

CHAPTERS 38-39

GOD BREAKS HIS SILENCE

CHAPTERS 38-39

If you have ever watched any kind of superhero movie then you probably have a clear understanding of the general plot before the movie even begins. First, you get a kind of background into the lives of the major characters, then there's that very subtle transition into the basic storyline of the plot. Following a bit of dialogue and build-up of relations between the characters, you get 'the problem.' This 'problem' defines the whole movie. Every emotion and action that follows is a consequence of this major problem that has presented itself in the lives of the characters. But, you know there's a superhero, and you know that this hero is bound to turn up. Now you're just left with one simple question: when?

This is a question Job pondered to himself all too often throughout the course of his suffering no doubt. "When will God, my Hero, show up? When will He break His lengthy silence?" Being the faithful man he was, Job knew God would not leave him stranded forever, but he wondered when He would come to deliver him. There is a famous quote by an unknown author: "God is never absent through the trials, only silent." Just like the teacher sitting silently while the students sit the test.

At the end of this test the students will seek the teacher out to get one thing – answers. Chapter 38 marks the inevitable end of God's silence when He finally comes to redeem Job. However God doesn't come possessing answers for Job, but rather questions. And these questions would come to represent the theme of this story. Before God can redeem Job, He must make him understand the magnitude of His works so that he can look back on his sufferings as a time of testing from God and not punishment. God doesn't do this by explaining the trials He allowed Job to experience but rather by reminding him of His work in creation.

It says that God chose to have this thought-provoking conversation with Job, "out of the whirlwind," (38:1). What is this whirlwind? St. John Chrysostom believes that God covered Job with clouds and whirlwinds; as though He came to talk to him "from above the mercy seat that was on the ark of the covenant from between the two cherubim" (Numbers 7: 89). This was done as a way to rebuke the friends of Job so that they would not bear witness to the secrets of God, and also to honor Job, that he would converse with God in a heavenly place. I feel as though this whirlwind is a symbol of the Church we have today. Sure, we are surrounded by people but when we come to the altar ready to partake of the Body and Blood of Christ, overcome by the clouds from the incense, we ultimately find ourselves personal witnesses to the secret treasures of God.

Chapter 38 continues with God asking Job questions regarding the creation of the

What the Fathers Say

As the cloud is a symbol of heaven, God intended for 'Job' to be put in heaven itself, and to come to him with His throne. It seems to me that the same thing happened when a dense cloud dwelt upon the Mount of Sinai (Exodus 19: 16); to let the children of Israel know that the voice is coming from high above.

– St. John Chrysostom

world, in essence asking, "were you there?"

"Were you there when I created the land, sea and all that is in them? Were you there when I made the clouds and the waters? Were you there when I created the light and made a path for the seas to travel through?"

CARING AND IN CONTROL

What God is trying to say by challenging Job to answer questions regarding the origin, size and nature of the world is that, "you, Job, are not in control, I am! I'm in control." Throughout the ordeal, Job tried to regain control by defending his innocence before his friends and by challenging God to answer his questions as to 'why' he was suffering. But here, God says, "I'm in control." Remember at the very beginning of the story, God was the one who gave Satan permission to attack Job? Does that mean He handed over control to the devil? Of course not! In fact, it is the opposite. God shows that He is in full control by allowing Job's sufferings, knowing with full confidence that Job would not utter a

People, Places &Things

Astronomy

Pleiades, Orion, Mazzaroth and the Great Bear all refer to a constellation of stars (see 38:31-32). These are all scientifically consistent with western knowledge today. Garrett P. Serviss, a noted astronomer, wrote about the bands of Orion in his book, Curiosities of

the Sky: "The great fi[g] of Orion appears to b[e] more lasting, not bec[ause] its stars are physicall[y] connected, but becaus[e] their great distance, [w] renders their moveme[nt] too deliberate to be e[asily] ascertained.

word against Him. The moment Job doubted that God was in control, God intervened. He reminds Job that he doesn't need to be in control, because God is the one who controls all the happenings of his life, asking, "Can you lift up your voice to the clouds, that an abundance of water may cover you?" (38:34). It is an extremely comforting thought to know that God is in control, even during times of trial. Why would I want to wrestle that control back from Him?

Following this, God reminds Job, again with a series of questions, that not only is He in control, but He cares! God cares about the happenings of the universe more than anyone else. He asks Job, "can you mark when the deer gives birth? (39:1). Who set the wild donkey free? (39:5). Have you given the horse strength? (39:19). Does the hawk fly by your wisdom? (39:26). And does the eagle mount up at your command? (39:27)." God reveals to Job that He cares about everything around him, things that we would often look at and think, 'well, who cares? Who cares what time the deer gives birth? It's not important so who cares?' The answer is: God cares. And so if God cares about such trivial little matters that concern animals, how much more will He care about things that concern His own special creation, us? Remember the Lord in the sermon on the mount comforting the multitudes and telling them, "Now if God so clothes the grass of the field, which today is, and tomorrow is thrown into the oven, will

> **What the Fathers Say**
>
> Who, while contemplating in the different nature of birds; how some of them have nice chirping voice; some have beautifully colored wings; and some, like eagles, soar up high, and seem to be standing still in the air; would not marvel to hear that the hawk "spread its wings toward the south." How could he then comprehend the works of the Creator of all?!
>
> – St. Cyril of Jerusalem

He not much more clothe you, O you of little faith?" (Mt 6:30).

By asking all these questions, God reminds Job of two very important facts of life. One, that He is in control. There is no point fighting for control of my own life when I realise that the Creator of the universe already has it. His ways are much higher than mine, so I need to trust in His dominion over my life. And two, He cares. God will never not care about even the most trivial of things in my life let alone the moments when I am truly suffering. Can you imagine your own parents walking by you while you are screaming in pain and telling you, "who cares about your pain?" Impossible! Their love for you is too great to leave you sitting there in pain. Just like God's love for Job was too great to leave him in his agony and suffering. It was high time the superhero made an appearance!

REFLECTION

Who is in control of my life? Am I able to let go of the reins and give God power in my life or do I have to be in command?

CHAPTERS 40-41

KNOW THYSELF

Events

CHAPTERS 40–41

Pretend you've been invited to the house of the Queen. It's been your dream for many years to meet her and finally, you've been extended a personal invite from her majesty herself. You stand silently as she makes her way into the room, you bow respectfully as she stands before you and then, she asks you a question. All the eyes in the room, the eyes of her guards, officials, special guests and her own all stare at you as you prepare yourself to speak to the Queen. What would be going through your mind? You are standing before royalty, and now you've been asked to speak to her. What do you say?

The truth is, whatever you prepared yourself to say you probably wouldn't. Standing before the Queen there is every chance you buckle and forget whatever it is you wanted to say to her. Why? Not because the opportunity has passed, but because it is in that moment, you realise who you are standing before. Now imagine the Queen in this story is God, and you, the one asked to speak to Him, are Job. This is the situation Job found himself in. And what did he say in response to the many questions God asked him, "Behold, I am vile" (40:4). The literal Hebrew translation of the word 'vile' is 'lightweight' or 'worthless.' Can you imagine that? Job, who complained against God for days, maybe weeks, was now face to face with Him and all he could say was, "I am worthless."

Why? Because it was in that moment that he realized who it was he stood before. God. The Creator of the world. How could he, in that moment, utter a single word against Him? It is, in fact, a lesson on repentance. The more time I spend in the presence of God, the more I will discover about myself. William Barclay once put it, "No man ever sees himself as he really is until he sees himself in the presence of Christ; and then he is appalled at the sight of himself." And Bede Griffith, a western monastic also said, in a very poetic way, "To discover God is not to discover an idea but to discover oneself. It is to awaken to that part of one's existence which has been hidden from sight and which one has failed to recognize. The discovery may be very painful; it is like going through a kind of death. But it is one thing which makes life worth living." It's like a man wearing dirty clothes walking into a spotlight. The closer he comes into the spotlight, the more he will be able to see the dirt that is on him.

It is not enough for me to just know who I am, I need to know who I am through Christ, through His presence. In a book titled 'The Greatest of all Sciences is to Know Thyself' by Anthony Coniaris, he states, "To 'know thyself' alone may mean that you sink into despair, but to 'know thyself' and find your true self in Christ is to find acceptance, forgiveness and power to rise above sin and despair to a new self, your true self, your best self." The most

What the Fathers Say

Tell God who you are; because if you do not, He will condemn you on what He finds in you. Do you want Him to forgive you? Say to Him: "Hide your face from my sins"; and, "I acknowledge my transgressions" (Psalm 51: 3, 9).

– St. Augustine

serious obstacle to reaching the truth about oneself, in his words, is pride or self-love. It is only once I forget myself and draw all my focus towards God and others that I begin to truly discover who I am.

THE BEHEMOTH AND LEVIATHAN

Following God's opening challenge for Job to recognize who he was, He then goes on to use two great animals, the Behemoth and Leviathan, to symbolize His total control over creation in correspondence with Job's helplessness. Of the Behemoth, the Lord says, "His bones are like beams of bronze, his ribs like bars of iron," (40:18) revealing how powerful this large creature was. Then He goes on to say, "He is the first of the ways of God; Only He who made him can bring near His sword" (40:19). God mentions this to show Job, that even that which he thinks is uncontrollable, like a large beast which powerfully roams the earth, God has the power to bring under control, into His

People, Places &Things

Behemoth & Leviathin

The word 'behemoth' is the plural word for 'livestock' (see Gen. 2:20). This plural form is frequently used for beasts of the field or woods. Leviathan is mentioned once as signifying a normal sea creature (Psa. 104:26) and three times in a more symbolic manner (Job 3:8;

Isa. 27:1 and Psa. 74. While both of these w can be used in a varie ways, several context factors in Job chapter & 41 favour understa behemoth and leviath two 'real' animals tha may have witnessed.

submission. Some fathers believe that the behemoth represents Satan, and this would make sense, that even though Satan has the capacity to instill chaos in our lives, God still has control over him and can bring to peace the disorder he has introduced into our lives.

The second beast spoken of by God is the Leviathan, a large sea creature (or dragon) of unknown identity. He begins by asking Job, "can you draw out Leviathan with a hook, or snare his tongue with a line which you lower?" (41:1). It is in this way that God rebukes 'Job', who more than once, tried to stand before Him, face to face, to debate Him, concerning the sufferings he went through. Here, God presents to Job several questions about the Leviathan, revolving around one point: If you cannot confront the horrible and most fearful creature in the sea, and catch him, how dare you seek to confront the Creator of this creature? If no man can confront the horrible Leviathan, the river dragon, who can destroy the life of man; and who symbolizes the devil, the true enemy of man, without support from God; how then can he enter a confrontation against God Himself, the Grantor of conquest to man? How can he even against the devil, and all his hosts?

It is perhaps at this point that Job realized where his true battle lies. His battle did not lie with God; his battle was with himself and the peace that had been robbed of him by the devil. All too often we turn to God to blame him for our 'unfair' or 'painful' circumstances. It is important to remember, God is on our side, He won't depart from us. It is us who have strayed not Him. Sometimes we can only discover this reality when we stand in His presence and realize who He is.

REFLECTION

Do I take time each evening to reflect on my day, week, month, year; and identify areas in my life that need change?

CHAPTER 42

CHAPTER 42

JOB RESTORED TO HIS GLORY!

Perhaps the most beautiful chapter in the entire book, chapter 42 explores the complete restoration of Job in light of his encounter with God. What we discover immediately is that, despite God's firm and harsh approach in dealing with Job, He still provided him with more comfort than any of His friends did – even though they did not raise their voice at him. We learn through this the importance of making God our first point of contact in life. Seldom do we approach God with a problem, or a fresh update on our lives before we go to our friends or family. We feel as though our friends are better equipped to respond to our needs than the God of Heaven is. In doing so we ignore one certain detail: God is our friend too! Imagine the way you speak to a friend and ask yourself, "do I speak to God that way too?" We get so caught up in the formalities of prayer, but God wants us to speak to Him as honestly as we speak to our friends. He wants to hear our complaints, He wants to rejoice with our successes in life, He wants to cry with us through our failures and He even wants to hear about the jokes that made us laugh. We need to try to speak to God as our friend, to talk to Him with deep sincerity and to speak openly with Him about anything; believing with full confidence that no friend on Earth can provide us with as much comfort as our Friend in Heaven. He is the best Friend we sometimes don't even realise we have!

ENCOUNTERING GOD

The question that arose from the very beginning of our study of Job until now is this: "Why does God allow good people to suffer?" Each character in this story had their own answer to this in regards to the righteous Job. His friends assumed that God is just and so Job must have sinned in his heart or by some other means to be deserving of his tribulations. To which Job responded saying that he was innocent of any wrong doing and that it was in fact God who was being unjust towards him. We presume that when God shows up He will finally provide an answer to this moral dilemma but, just as we saw in the whirlwind, He doesn't. Had God answered this question would Job feel comforted in any way? Perhaps. But picture this scenario: a woman hears that her teenage son has been killed in a car accident. When she asks the police officer how, or why, he was killed, the police officer replies, "the driver of the car was drunk." Does the answer to her question

Job

The name Job has two meanings. In Hebrew, the name means, "the persecuted one," whereas in Arabic it means, "the repentant one." This is fitting with the character development of Job throughout the book as he struggles with persecution until he reaches a point of deep repentance.

People, Places & Things

give her peace of mind? No, because it does nothing for the pain she feels at the loss of her dear son. God in His infinite wisdom knows this and so offers Job something much sweeter – Himself. His presence to Job was the ultimate comfort. Job expected that God would come to tell him that "his suffering is not to be compared with what He is preparing for him in the age to come" (Rom 8:18); But for God to appear and transfigure before him, and to talk to him, that was something beyond his wildest dreams! He says: "I have heard of You by the hearing of the ear, but now my eye sees You" (42: 5) in the most honest and beautiful words to come out of his mouth. Words he yearned to say his whole life as he built his relationship with God. Almost as though he is saying, "I have heard about You, how You created the world and how You deliver Your people, but in seeing You Lord, You have satisfied the deepest aching of my heart!" Just as Moses asked to see the glory of God on Mt Sinai (Exodus 33:18), the most any man could desire in this life, is to come face to face with God. What is most beautiful about seeing God in the whirlwind is that Job can conclude that he no longer needs an explanation, for the presence of God is much sweeter.

This encounter with God drives him to "abhor himself, and repent in dust and ashes," (42:6). To defend himself before his friends, Job proclaimed his righteousness, in contrast to those around him. Now in the light of God's holiness, he sees himself as nothing, and discovers that he is indeed corrupted. Likewise with us, we must also bring ourselves into the Light of Christ in order to illuminate our faults, flaws and transgressions. We must recognize with King David that "our goodness is nothing apart from the Lord," (Ps 16:2) and that we are in constant need of drawing nearer to Him so that our hidden sins may be exposed for us to live a life of continual repentance.

SILENT SUFFERING

To say that God exalted Job and elevated his status to one that was far greater than before his tribulations began, may well be an understatement. To appreciate this understatement, let us see what the Lord does to those who persecute His servants. He says to Eliphaz, the eldest of Job's friends, "My wrath is aroused against you and your two friends, for you have not spoken of Me what is right, as My servant Job has" (42: 7)." Not only that, but he tells them to ask Job to intercede for them! Can you imagine their humiliation? For so long Job tried to plead with his friends to heed his voice but they wouldn't listen – they denied him of his innocence. But God is the defender of the righteous and in our time of trial, He will testify for us. Sometimes it is better for us to remain silent in the face of false accusation, our pleas will doubtless fall on deaf ears. If we suffer in silence, in prayer and supplication to the Lord, He will come in His acceptable time and deliver us from our opponents. In Lamentations it says of the

Do you see what it means to give something for the sake of God? It means that you will be restored twice as much as you gave; and even as said by the gospels: "shall receive a hundredfold and inherit everlasting life" (Matthew 19: 29), in Christ Jesus.

– Origen

youthful man facing tribulation, "let him sit alone and keep silent because God has laid it on him," (Lam 3:28). This speaks prophetically of our Lord Christ who Himself was silent before His accusers, though understood that one day He would be vindicated, telling them, "hereafter you will see the Son of Man sitting at the right hand of the Power, and coming on the clouds of Heaven," (Matt 26:64).

The lesson: stay silent in the face of accusation, trust that God will come to your defense.

Finally, after the grand suffering of Job, we read the words we have been waiting for, "And the Lord restored Job's losses when he prayed for his friends," (42:10). Notice how Job was restored not after his repentance alone, but after he interceded for his friends in a spirit of forgiveness. In the Arabic translation of the verse it says that "The Lord restored Job's (captivity) when he prayed for his friends" and so, Fr Tadros Yacoub Malaty puts it perfectly saying that "he has enjoyed the inner freedom, when he raised up his heart, mind, as well as his hands, for the sake of his adversaries, to ask the Lord to forgive them. There is no way to enjoy freedom, other than to open our hearts by love; not only toward our beloved ones and relatives, but even toward our opponents and adversaries." Ask yourself honestly, do you pray for your persecutors? The Lord encourages us to "love our enemies, bless those who curse us, do good to those who hate us and pray for those who spitefully use and persecute us," (Matt 5:44). It doesn't seem practical or even possible, but I think if the story of Job is any indication, it offers us a promise from God – that we would enjoy a freedom in Christ that instills within us a divine peace. And if that isn't enough of a promise, the Lord goes on to say, "that you be sons of your Father in Heaven," (Matt 5:45).

REFLECTION

Do I make time to thank God for everything, both the good and the bad, in my life, or am I too busy complaining about my pain?

CONCLUSION

That's it. You made it. We are finally at the end of this toilsome story. Now it's time to breathe and for one final time, let us return to the question: "why does God allow for suffering in this world?" There are many answers, some say to build character, some to build patience, some for correction – and all these carry an element of truth. However, through reading the story of Job, there is perhaps a definitive answer to this question – so that we may be found by Him.

Picture a little child who runs away from home and gets lost in the woods. After many days of travelling alone, the child will inevitably get hungry, tired, cold and worst of all, lost. If the child finds food, he solves the immediate problem of his hunger, but all the other problems will remain. If he finds shelter, he may solve both his tiredness and cold, but he is still hungry and lost. However, if the child's Father searches for him and finds him, the child becomes no longer lost, but found. No doubt the Father, seeing His child hungry, tired and cold will look at him and say, "Let's go get you something to eat," or "Let's get you out of those clothes and get you warm." Christ Himself promises this when he tells the story of the return of the Prodigal Son. Being found by Christ is not an immediate solution to all our problems, but with Him, all our problems pale to insignificance, because I can now go through them with Him.

CONCLUSION

It can then be concluded that God allows us to suffer so that we may learn to invite His presence into our lives, "that the genuineness of your faith, being much more precious than gold that perishes, though it is tested by fire, may be found to praise, honor and glory at the revelation of Jesus Christ," (1 Pet. 1:7).

Glory be to God Amen.

Printed in the USA
CPSIA information can be obtained
at www.ICGtesting.com
LVHW050546090224
771078LV00003B/466